POSTERS OF

WORLD WAR I AND WORLD WAR II

IN THE GEORGE C. MARSHALL

RESEARCH FOUNDATION

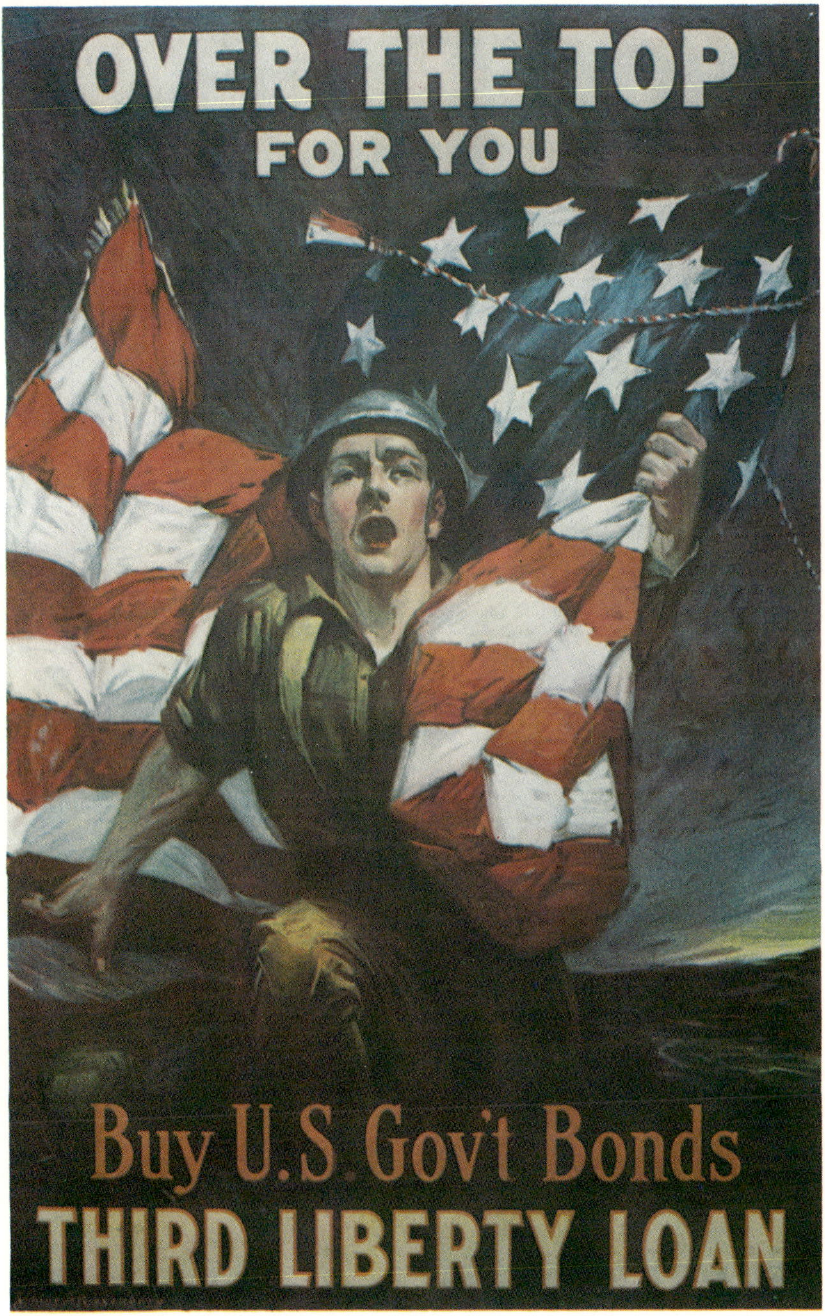
OVER THE TOP
FOR YOU
Buy U.S. Gov't Bonds
THIRD LIBERTY LOAN

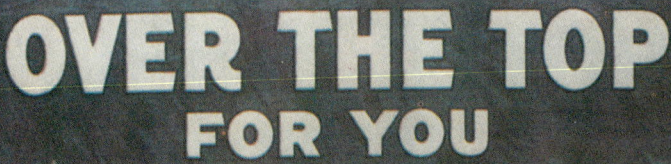

Posters of World War I and World War II in the George C. Marshall Research Foundation

Anthony R. Crawford, Editor

with an introduction by

O. W. Riegel

A George C. Marshall Research Foundation Publication
The University Press of Virginia, Charlottesville

POSTERS OF WORLD WAR I AND WORLD WAR II IN THE GEORGE C. MARSHALL RESEARCH FOUNDATION. Copyright © 1979 by The George C. Marshall Research Foundation. All rights reserved. No part of this book may be reproduced in any manner whatsoever without written permission except in the case of brief quotations embodied in critical articles and reviews. For information address The George C. Marshall Research Foundation, Drawer 920, Lexington, Virginia 24450.

Library of Congress Cataloging in Publication Data:

George C. Marshall Research Foundation.
    Posters of World War I and World War II in the George C. Marshall Research Foundation.

    "A George C. Marshall Research Foundation publication."
    1. European War, 1914-1918—Posters—Catalogs.
    2. World War, 1939-1945—Posters—Catalogs.
    3. George C. Marshall Research Foundation—Catalogs.
    I. Crawford, Anthony R.   II. Title.

D522.25.G46 1979   016.769'4'99403   79-9852
ISBN 0-8139-0778-0

Printed in the United States of America

CONTENTS

Foreword	vii
Preface	ix
Introduction	1
Posters	17
Inventory	43
World War I	
Canada	46
France	46
Great Britain	53
United States	60
World War II	
Canada	70
France	73
Germany	73
Great Britain	97
United States	98
Index Of Artists	125

Foreword

The George C. Marshall Research Foundation is a unique living memorial to one of the key leaders of our country. Its program is devoted to the study of those areas of activity in which General Marshall distinguished himself, ranging generally from the period of World War I through his last public service as secretary of defense at the time of the Korean War.

The archives of the Foundation include the personal papers of General Marshall, documents relating to his life and work, the papers of many of his associates, thousands of photographs, and—of special interest to students of propaganda—an important collection of posters from the periods of the First and Second World Wars.

It is this last collection which is cataloged and illustrated in this publication. Benefiting from a National Endowment for the Arts grant and directed by the archivist, Anthony R. Crawford, this guide owes much to O. W. Riegel, Professor Emeritus, Washington and Lee University; David Coffey, project assistant; Larry and Joellen Bland, typesetting and make-up; Sally Mann, photographer; and Maria Colvin, translator. The Foundation is proud to expand knowledge of this collection in this manner and to add, thereby, to its central purpose as a regional and national research institution.

Fred L. Hadsel, Director
George C. Marshall Research Foundation

Preface

The Marshall Foundation's poster collection has been established over the last twenty years through the generosity of individual donors who have collectively made this catalog possible. The majority of the posters were donated by Ian H. Ackroyd-Kelly in memory of Walter H. Ackroyd-Kelly (on indefinite loan through the courtesy of the Virginia Military Institute Museum), George Blow, Hélen Hill Miller, Forrest C. Pogue and Melvin Ryder. Other donors include: Lelia Cocke Bagbey; Mrs. M. S. Battle; Arthur L. Buck; Leigh B. Hanes, Jr. in memory of John D. Guthrie; Catherine Bemiss McGuire; Preston Library, Virginia Military Institute; O. W. Riegel; Marie Marshall Singer and Otis D. Smith.

For some time the Marshall Foundation has been involved in a project utilizing its World War I and World War II posters to enable its staff to preserve the collection and to make it available in several formats to students and scholars interested in studying and researching the numerous subjects and aspects unique to war posters. This catalog is the culmination of that undertaking and serves as a description and guide to the nearly seven hundred war posters in the collection. The project has been carried out in three major phases: photographing, accessioning and processing, and catalog preparation.

A color slide and a black and white photograph and negative have been produced of each poster in the collection. These are available for research use in the Marshall Foundation, and reprints can be purchased by individuals.

The posters have been accessioned and stored for preservation according to the numbering system of the inventory at the end of this volume. The color slides and the black and white photographs and negatives have also been filed under the inventory number.

This volume consists of three sections. An introduction by O. W. Riegel—propaganda analyst for the Office of War Information in World War II and former head, Department of Journalism and Communications, Washington and Lee University—describes the uniqueness of the collection and discusses how posters were used as propaganda during wartime. The photographic reproductions represent examples from the collection and illustrate the themes discussed in the introduction. Finally, the inventory contains a descriptive entry for each poster in the collection and guides the user to the location of the original poster in the archives and to its counterpart in the photograph and slide file.

The Marshall Foundation wishes to acknowledge the valuable contributions to the project and the catalog of O. W. Riegel, for the introduction and his advice during the project, and of David Coffey for his research and photographic work as project assistant during this undertaking. The photographs used as catalog illustrations are the work of Sally Mann. Valuable technical assistance in preparing the manuscript for publication was provided by Larry and Joellen Bland. Maria Colvin donated much time and effort in translating the German posters. The assistance provided by the Washington and Lee University journalism department is also appreciated, in particular that of Professor John K. Jennings and journalism majors Mark Richard and William G. Hyland. The project could not have been carried through without the encouragement of Royster Lyle, Jr., Associate Director of the Marshall Foundation. Finally, without the financial assistance of the National Endowment for the Arts, Washington, D.C., the entire project and this catalog would not have been possible.

Anthony R. Crawford, Archivist
George C. Marshall Research Foundation

POSTERS OF

WORLD WAR I AND WORLD WAR II

IN THE GEORGE C. MARSHALL

RESEARCH FOUNDATION

Introduction

Posters of World War I and World War II
in the George C. Marshall Research Foundation

O. W. Riegel

The poster collection of the Marshall Foundation complements its other holdings by illustrating another important facet of the two world wars in which General Marshall served and by illuminating the social changes that occurred during his lifetime.

The posters appeal to a variety of interests. They may be seen as history, chronicling the First and Second World Wars, reflecting the changing needs, anxieties, and hopes of the warring nations as well as turns in the tides of battle. They may be seen as propaganda—a lexicon of devices, appeals and psychological stratagems to marshal peoples, to woo friends, and to confound enemies. They may be viewed as sociology, reflecting the popular culture, mores, prejudices, vocabulary, and stereotyped images of their times. Or they may be viewed simply for their own visual sake, sometimes inspiring, sometimes funny or crude, but always fascinating.

What Is a Poster?

The poster has affinities with store signs, paintings on walls, art prints, display advertising, commercial flyers, and the like. As generally understood, however, and as used in this publication, the poster denotes a form of graphic presentation in which all of the following elements are present: (1) it is cheaply produced in multiple copies, usually on paper, and usually in a combination of text and picture; (2) it is intended for public display (posters are for posting); and (3) it contains a message that is intended to move or to persuade the viewer.

The poster has become so commonplace that people may now grow up unaware of its comparatively recent origin. Although in earlier times a limited number of copies could be made from engravings on wood and metal, before the nineteenth century art was mainly a matter of one-of-a-kind wall or easel painting available only to the wealthy or affixed to the walls of churches and castles. A technical breakthrough occurred late in the eighteenth century when a Bavarian, Aloys Senefelder, somewhat accidentally discovered lithography. According to one story, Senefelder, not finding a piece of paper handy, wrote his laundry list with a greasy pencil on a piece of flat limestone, and later found the list imprinted on the laundry he had thrown on the stone.

Artists utilized the discovery both to develop a new art form and to increase their income through the sale of multiple copies, and this led eventually to an unprecedented democratization and diffusion of art at a time of industrialization and rapid population growth. Refinements in the technology of planography (printing from flat surfaces) kept pace with this growth, from the cumbersome lithograph stone to the zinc plate and through other developments to the present methods of offset photolithography on high-speed presses. The social effects of this technology roughly paralleled those of another new technology, the photograph. Formerly, the painted family portrait or landscape and the statue were the exclusive privilege of a few wealthy owners. Photography made the likeness and the image available to virtually everyone.

The commercial world quickly recognized the utility of lithography for reaching mass-consuming publics, and by the middle of the nineteenth century—from a union of technology and salesmanship—the modern poster emerged as a new medium of communication and as, literally, a visual addition to the landscape. Along with other technological inventions and advances such as electricity, the automobile, electronics, assembly lines, and mass marketing, the poster took its place as a characteristic sight, product, and function of new mass-production, consuming societies.

As effective communication, the poster had a number of things going for it. Most obvious was the eye-catching picture, communicable even to the illiterate. Another was the tradition of the proclamation (fig. 1).[1] For centuries portentous and authoritative announcements had been posted in public places. A king's levy of troops and Martin Luther's theses are examples. Words in print had prestige and authority, especially when printed large. And, until well into the twentieth century, there was no other effective means for communicating to large numbers of people—no radio and no television—with the exception of newspapers and other printed matter which had relatively limited circulations and impact.

A disadvantage of the poster was the disdain in which it was held by many because of its commercialization by journeyman illustrators to

---

[1] Numbers in parentheses throughout the introduction refer to the figure numbers given the illustrations reproduced in this book, beginning on page 17.

promote such products as bicycles and soap. This attitude began to change when first-rate artists entered the field; the Toulouse-Lautrec *affiches* for the Moulin Rouge and Alfons Mucha's posters for Sarah Bernhardt are well-known examples. By the beginning of the twentieth century the poster was established as a component of the art world; poster collecting became a fad, and special journals for poster collectors appeared.

The Marshall Collection in Perspective

The World War I posters in the Marshall Foundation collection represent a landmark in poster history—the first large-scale use of the poster for political purposes. It was inevitable that national governments should embrace the poster as a primary instrument for mobilizing their peoples for war and appropriate that a democratized art should be employed in a new kind of "democratized" war: that is, war that involved entire populations, civil as well as military.

It may not be excessive to say that the poster campaign involving all warring nations during World War I has never been equaled in its combination of magnitude and poster primacy for a single cause. As many—or more—posters may have been issued during World War II, but their impact was subordinate to domestic and shortwave radio and to a variety of other propaganda instruments that included the airborne leaflet and the clandestine newspaper. By World War II also, most countries were saturated with inexpensive newspapers and magazines, reducing dependence on the poster for mass communication.

In April of 1917 Charles Dana Gibson organized a division of pictorial publicity, comprised of artists who offered their services free of charge to the United States government. Some 700 posters were produced in the nineteen months of the division's existence. A similar group of volunteers served the United States Navy. In all, an estimated 2,000 to 3,000 posters were produced in the United States alone during World War I for government and civilian agencies, and printings of 100,000 were not uncommon. The most celebrated World War I poster, James Montgomery Flagg's finger-pointing Uncle Sam, "I Want You," was revived for World War II and has had subsequent printings, for a probable total of around 5,000,000 (fig. 2).

The example of World War I established the poster as a political instrument. Beginning with the 1920s, political parties in all developed countries adopted the poster for party recruiting and election campaigns.

Communist and National Socialist posters in Germany in the early thirties, Gaullist and Communist posters in France in the fifties, anti-Vietnam posters in the United States and posters of the French student revolt in the sixties, are examples of a by now virtually universal use of the poster for political ends.

Governments too have continued to employ the poster, not only for war (the Spanish civil war, Korea, and the recent wars in the Middle East are examples), but also for morale building and for instruction and indoctrination between wars. Some nations, such as the Soviet Union, the People's Republic of China, and Cuba, are "poster countries," which produce propaganda posters in remarkable quantity and variety for export as well as for domestic uses and which sell them (in the cases of the Soviet Union and China) in special poster shops.

The poster world is one of infinite variety, and its highlights and golden ages occur in response to the aspirations and means of sponsoring power or pressure groups, the needs and interests of people, the inventiveness of artists, and the tastes of poster collectors. The commercial poster has had two golden ages, one in the twenties and thirties and one in the fifties, both in response to artists' innovations in graphics and the state of the consumer market. Certain categories of posters, such as travel, motion-picture and art-exhibition posters, are often superb in execution—and each has a coterie of collectors.

As the last quarter of the twentieth century begins, the poster world is changing. The use of the poster by its most potent and affluent sponsors, governments and commerce, appears to have reached a plateau or even to have diminished. Some believe this is because television is considered a more effective means in terms of unit cost, for reaching mass audiences. On the other hand, new do-it-yourself technologies for the reproduction of posters in large quantities—such as the silk-screen process and the small photolitho presses installed in offices, living rooms, and classrooms—have resulted in a proliferation of posters sponsored by environmentalists, civil libertarians, antimilitarists, fringe groups of the political left and right, and other minorities. Such groups usually have little access to television, because of both a lack of money and policies or restrictions of the station or network. Television in most countries is government operated and is inaccessible to movements and ideas not in harmony with government policy. Posters produced during the student revolt in France in 1968 at the Beaux-Arts and in classrooms are examples of unorthodox posters of dissent. Usually small in size and often crude, they are at the same time often innovative in design, with arresting messages.

Faddism is another cause of recent deviations from the classic standards of the poster. The psychedelic poster of the 1960s and 1970s, for example, a popular fixture of college dormitory rooms and discotheques, may promote a certain life-style, but it is more a decoration than a message displayed in a public place to move or persuade. Another nonposter (according to the traditional definition of the poster) is the reproduction in our time of celebrated or quaint World War I posters, which are no longer functional but have become decorative *objets d'art*. As in the cases of the spinning wheel and the ship's lantern, functional obsolescence over the years has created aesthetic values in old posters that they did not previously possess.

Posters and War

War posters of all countries and times are remarkably similar in their basic messages. Once a nation is committed to war, it endeavors by every available means to promote enthusiasm for the war, to enhance the morale (and therefore the effectiveness) of the fighting forces, to exhort its people to make and accept sacrifices and deprivations, and, when possible, to discourage the enemy and cause him to despair. Every nation portrays its warriors as noble (fig. 3), its women as compassionate and virtuous (fig. 4), its war aims as righteous (fig. 5). The enemy, on the contrary, is portrayed as misguided, evil, fighting for an ignoble cause (fig. 6). If the language of any war poster were translated and a few changes made in costume and symbol, it often would be difficult to tell in what country that poster originated or in what war (figs. 7, 8).

Nevertheless, there are indeed differences in style, stress and symbol and vocabulary between the war posters of different nations. There are also differences between wars. Not all World War I and World War II posters are interchangeable, although most are.

In the broad view, the function of the war poster is to make coherent and acceptable a basically incoherent and irrational ordeal of killing, suffering, and destruction that violates every accepted principle of morality and decent living. This requires ingenuity and skill, as well as a predisposition of the audience to believe.

World War I

World War I, a war of rival imperialisms and a war that was "to be over by Christmas," needed only one poster for its beginning on the European continent. This was the mobilization order for conscripts. By Christmas the war had become a stalemate that was to continue through four years of carnage and attrition. During much of that time, the front lines of trenches moved hardly more than ten miles. To sustain this unexpected kind of war, the poster was enlisted to raise money (fig. 9), to provide aid and comfort for the troops (fig. 10), to encourage the saving of essentials (fig. 11), to create sympathy for the relief of the victims of war (fig. 12), to maintain the morale of the populace (fig. 13), and to promote the productivity of labor to feed the war machine (fig. 14).

The exception at the beginning was Great Britain, where there had been no conscription and where, until conscription was introduced eighteen months later, a vast campaign was launched to raise an army of a million by voluntary enlistment. To this end, a stream of posters appealed to the patriotism of British males of military age, called them to their "duty," cajoled them, and finally, sought to shame them into enlisting (fig. 15). With conscription, the problems and posters of Great Britain evolved along the same lines as those of the continental countries.

In the United States, the declaration of war on April 6, 1917, had been preceded by a national preparedness campaign, with posters, and by large-scale recruiting campaigns by the military services, also with posters. With the declaration of war, the stream of posters became a deluge. On April 14, the Women's Suffrage Party, aided by battalions of Boy Scouts, plastered New York City with 20,000 recruiting posters. Gibson's division of pictorial publicity was organized the same month. Among the prominent artists who made posters and are represented in the Marshall collection are the Americans Flagg, Howard Chandler Christy, Haskell Coffin, Joseph Leyendecker, and Joseph Pennell (fig. 16), and the French Jules Abel Faivre, Maurice Neumon, Francisque Poulbot, and Lucien-Hector Jonas.

In the overall view, the posters of the First World War were exhortations that sought to exploit people's conscious or subconscious vulnerabilities to appeals to basic emotions of self-preservation, tribal patriotic pride, and traditional morality. The simplistic poster was not the place for the new and unfamiliar in either word or art. Nor was it a vehicle for reasoned arguments on the causes of the war, its strategy, or its probable results—if an intelligent explanation of the war were possible. Posters had to have a "modern" look or to evoke a national nostalgic memory, but in either case their appeal was to familiar ideas and images, conventional wisdom, and a simplified perception of war as right versus wrong.

Typically, these ends were accomplished by employing the following methods (and the same devices were used again in the posters of the Second World War).

1. Images of national leaders past and present, or quotations from those leaders, or both (fig. 17—with Robert E. Lee, George Washington and Stonewall Jackson in the background): such posters exalted the leader like icons and employed his prestige to legitimatize the war and to unify the population behind him and his cause in the spirit of obedience and faith. The ultimate example of this device occurred, of course, not in World War I, but in World War II in Germany, in the person of Adolph Hitler (fig. 18).

2. Symbols: Every nation has its vocabulary of idiosyncratic image and word—such as the national anthem, coat of arms, bird (fig. 19), Red Cross (fig. 20), flag (fig. 21), flower, or terms like "Valley Forge" and "Liberty"—that instantly evokes feelings of patriotism or sympathy, short circuits to emotion. Some symbols are virtually universal, such as the Christian cross (fig. 22), the eagle (fig. 23), the lion (fig. 24), and the snake (fig. 25). Some are old, and some emerge during the course of the wars, such as the Red Cross nurse (fig. 26), and the "V" for victory of World War II (fig. 27). The standby in all wars is the mystique of "my country"—nation, *patrie, heimat, vaterland, otechestvo, patria,* "blighty" (figs. 28, 29)—magical words that may be relied upon to produce a reflex of huddling together in time of fear and of exalting together in time of triumph. All successful symbols have two things in common: they stand for complex abstractions, and they defy rational explanation.

3. Slogans: "Beat Back the Hun" (fig. 30), "Remember Belgium" (fig. 31), and "Greatest Mother in the World" are typical of the magical phrases that abound in wartime posters and become part of our collective memory, whether we like it or not. "The World Cannot Live Half Slave and Half Free"—a proposition palpably untrue (one need only look around)—was launched into the national consciousness by Lincoln, appropriated for posters in the First World War, and revived for the posters of the Second World War. The French revolutionary slogan of 1792, *On les aura* ("We'll get them"), was re-echoed in the First and Second World Wars, each time with new accretions of historical association and sentiment (figs. 32, 33).

4. Myths, allegories, and metaphors: These are forms of symbol, evoking a familiar folk story, a classical myth, a national memory, an idealiz-

ed personification (fig. 34), or cause-and-effect relationships standardized by education or habitual and orthodox ways of thinking—the hammer and the anvil (fig. 35), Joan of Arc, savior of France (fig. 36), Saint George and the dragon.

5. Semiotic illustration: An idea is reinforced in a picture by stance and gesture, facial expression, costume, and appropriate action (fig. 37). Design itself may be semiotic, as between dynamic diagonals and passive horizontals, or between aspiring verticals and serene ovals. In the more successful posters, words too are designed and integrated for the total effect (fig. 38).

6. Countermeans: All of the devices above can also be used in reverse to vilify and degrade the enemy and to combat sabotage, noncooperation, and apathy. The enemy leaders are portrayed as monstrous, the enemy soldier as villainous or pathetic. Caricature and ridicule may be used. It should be noted that in the First World War the British and Americans were more inclined to use this kind of malevolent propaganda (Lord Northcliffe and his atrocity propaganda is an example) than the French. The Germans used it hardly at all.

In the light of postwar disillusionment caused by the appalling slaughter in World War I and by revelations of the vanity, chicanery, and stupidity of many of the war leaders (General Sir Douglas Haig is an example), it is especially ironic that the posters conceal the realities of the war behind a fog of propaganda. The political and military leaders are always portrayed as selfless and brilliant saviors of the nation, beyond reproach. The soldiers are always brave, humane, and without moral stain, presumably preserving their chastity until they return home to their wives and sweethearts. Refugees are always innocent women and small children. Soldiers on the battlefield may detain the enemy with a rifle or thrust a bayonet at the enemy or fire a machine gun into the horizon, but seldom is someone shown actually being killed or maimed within the poster (fig. 39), especially during the early period of the war. Corpses are sometimes shown on the battlefield, but they are impersonal and vaguely defined. As for the wounded, a few posters show handsome men who have been blinded. One poster has a soldier with his arm in a sling as well as patches over his eyes, being led by a Red Cross nurse, but we may assume that the Red Cross is restoring him to health (fig. 40). The French were somewhat more realistic than the British and Americans, however, in portrayals of battle scenes and the wounded (fig. 41).

Women have been a mainstay of the poster from the beginning: to catch the eye; to drench the poster with an aura of the traditional feminine attributes of grace, beauty, appealing defenselessness, and moral virtue; and to sell goods and causes. The World War I poster is a showcase for the portrayal of the *femme* as *objet*. Typically, she is shown in a white uniform or voluminous and stately robes as a figure of compassion (fig. 42); or in a gossamer dress of classical line, blessing or leading the battle (fig. 43); or, in startling contrast, as a sweet gray homemaker, everybody's grandmother (fig. 44). In this case, too, there were some national differences: American women, for example, were prettier; French women, more realistic and credible. Children are also appealing poster subjects in every war (fig. 45). In World War II, as we shall see, there were also to be some changes in the feminine image.

World War II

If World War I could be called a war of rival imperialisms, World War II could be called a war of rival nationalisms and ideologies, triggered by authoritarians with extravagant ambitions. Quite different militarily from World War I's static furnace of destruction, World War II was a war of movement on land, sea, under the sea, and in the air; was fought over great distances in various parts of the world, engulfing whole nations and creating millions of refugees; and was decided ultimately by the greater ability of one side to produce more—and more effective— equipment and weapons for this kind of war. It was also many times more destructive than World War I, with its conservatively estimated ten million military deaths and twenty million wounded. During World War II there were at least thirty million military deaths alone and additional millions of civilian deaths from bombings, death camps, and starvation, and there were uncounted millions of military and civilian wounded.

It is ironic, considering the ideological issues of World War II (fascism, communism, democracy, and capitalism were some of the ideologies in conflict) and its greater scope and cruelty, that its posters were generally not as fervent, emotional, or compelling as those of World War I. This is a subjective judgment, of course, difficult to measure and open to argument. Several factors, however, may account for the differences in character, functions, and impact of the posters of World War II as compared with those of World War I.

One of these factors was a new sophistication regarding the poster and propaganda in general that followed, and was partly a result of, World War I. Postwar disillusionment, the exposure of the frauds of atrocity propaganda, the work of Freud and his followers on human psychological susceptibilities, and the writings of revisionist historians had all had the effect of creating a consciousness of propaganda and of regarding it as an evil. This suspicion and hostility led to the idea that propaganda was most effective when it was "least propagandistic." According to this view, many World War I posters were naive in their patriotic exuberance and were merely laughable in a more sophisticated age.

Nevertheless, the use of the poster was not abandoned. On the contrary, it was cultivated by commercial interests and increasingly by political parties and national governments, but with a more sophisticated regard for public taste and tolerance and for the creditability level of various poster appeals.

A second factor was the appearance by the time of World War II of a variety of new and promising propaganda weapons and strategies. The Soviet Union, to consolidate domestic power and for self-defense, was a pioneer in the propaganda use of medium and shortwave radio, film (which Lenin especially favored), wall newspapers, public loud-speakers, and the agitation and propaganda activities of the Communist International. Germany soon followed aggressively with a powerful radio broadcasting complex at Zeesen, a program of domestic regimentation and indoctrination, and a network of German nationals and sympathizers around the world that was to become popularly known as the fifth column, a term that first came into use during the Spanish Civil War of 1936-39. The Western democracies, having no comparable political ambitions or urgencies, lagged in the development of the new communications instruments. They possessed the technologies and skills, however, and when they entered the war they were quickly able to launch propaganda operations on a vast scale.

The new media—especially radio—along with much more efficient facilities than during World War I for gathering, distributing, and publishing information, tended to subordinate and reduce the importance, in a relative sense, of the poster. Moreover, radio, clandestine newspapers and postcards, airborne leaflets and newspapers, and leaflet artillery shells made possible for the first time a substantial direct propaganda assault upon enemy military and civilian populations. The poster was unsuitable for propaganda behind enemy lines, although there was some clandestine poster activity by the resistance and posters played an important role in areas occupied and liberated by the Allied forces.

A third factor is more difficult to define and pertains mainly to the Anglo-Saxon democracies, which—because the Allied countries in Western Europe were occupied or under German control—produced most of the posters for the Allied side except for the Soviet Union. As much as Hitler and Mussolini and the Japanese warlords were detested, there was at the same time a certain reserve in the West toward a war that was generally considered necessary but unsought, and had been entered into with a kind of grim fatalism without heroics. Also, engendered by the failure of peace efforts and the League of Nations between the wars, there was a certain skepticism regarding the probable results of the war, an absence of great expectations for what would follow the destruction of the Axis. In the United States a special inhibiting influence arose from a long tradition of popular hostility toward government-sponsored propaganda in any form. All of the factors above may account for a diminution of the exuberance and crusading zeal that characterized the posters of the First World War.

The means and themes of World War II posters repeated those of the First World War, as previously described, with certain variations and additions.

Appeals for production and conservation included a wider range of subjects and activities in the United States, from factories and farming (fig. 46) to travel (fig. 47) and protecting forests from fire—reflecting the expanded size and organization of the country (fig. 48). On the unity theme, posters recognized the contributions of the black and ethnic minorities (fig. 49).

Women did not lose their femininity, but were portrayed trimmer and more businesslike, usually at work in factory (fig. 50) or shipyard or in the uniform of one of the new military branches for women. The goddesses in sheer shifts, the soubrettes with flashing eyes, and the folksy mothers and grandmothers yielded to the career woman.

The handling of ideology was neither subtle nor profound, consisting mainly of attacks upon the cruelty and godlessness of Nazism and warlords (fig. 51) and affirmations of traditional American principles of God-fearing piety, good works, and humane intentions (fig. 52). Socioeconomic ideas were avoided by the conservative Western allies, and Communism, in deference to our Soviet ally, was never mentioned. The German tocsin at the specter of Bolshevism went unanswered in the American poster.

Appeals for money emphasized self-interest to a great extent, whereas World War I posters had stressed sympathy and succor for starving refugees and other embattled European victims of war. Concerning conservation too, the stress was on self-interest—for a full stomach in a warm, contented home, with little or no reference to the plight of the peoples of Europe (fig. 53). There were, however, private organizations that raised money for the relief of refugees and war victims of various countries (fig. 54).

A speciality of World War II was the poster to stop careless talk. Employed by both sides in the war, it flourished in the Anglo-Saxon nations with notable variety and ingenuity, in motifs ranging from the deeply tragic to the comic caricature (figs. 55, 56). The rationale of the careless-talk campaigns was the importance of logistics, troop and material transportation, and the secret development of new weapons in an age of rapid electronic communication, but whether the practical results were commensurate with the magnitude of the poster effort is an unanswered question.

Unlike the posters of World War I, the use of photographs was common in the posters of World War II. From the point of view of art, posters of the Second World War were skillful and competent, but it is difficult to think of any that were as memorable as the French and some American and German posters of the First World War. As in 1917-18, prominent artists contributed posters, Thomas Hart Benton and Ben Shahn, among others. Important American poster makers included Stevan Dohanes, Norman Rockwell, Albert Dorne, McClelland Barclay, Jean Carlu, and J. W. Schlaikjer (fig. 57), all represented in the Marshall collection.

Several examples in World War II posters suggest a somewhat greater realism than in World War I in the depiction of the nature of war (fig. 58). More caricature and humor appeared, with the Axis leaders usually the butt of the joke (fig. 59).

In Germany the poster served the aims and tenets of national socialism with skill, force, and consistency. The major themes were the unity of the German people in obedience to the infallible leader, Adolf Hitler (fig. 60); pride in both the German people and the mystique of Germanism (fig. 61); the horror and danger of Bolshevism; the peril the Jew represented to racial purity; the corruption and weakness of democracies and their leaders; the invincibility of the righteous German cause (fig. 62); and the glory of sacrifice for Hitler, his *Reich,* and the German *volk.* As the German war effort progressed from triumph to defeat, the appeals increased in stridency, especially the call for heroic sacrifice (fig. 63). Germans were constantly reminded, sometimes with allusions to the exploits of Frederick the Great, that defeat could be turned at any moment into victory.

Allied propaganda to the Germans involved the poster hardly at all, but for purposes of background it may be noted that as the war progressed, Allied propaganda concentrated more and more, directly and by suggestion, upon the creation of defeatism, hopelessness, and despair in the Axis military and civilian populations. One poster example, produced by the Office of War Information for the Yugoslav resistance—for posting where the German occupiers might see it—shows a terrified German soldier walking alone at night through a sinister forest. The single-word caption is *Herrenvolk* (Master Race).

The posters that followed the Allied armies of liberation stressed unity, patriotism, and hope (fig. 64). Consolidation posters characteristically flattered liberated peoples. The posters imported into France in the wake of the Normandy invasion, for example, featured the French soldier or flag in the center, with British and American soldiers or flags on each side, or showed the French soldier or flag at a higher elevation (fig. 65). National symbols and heroes—in France, Marianne wearing the Phrygian cap of the Revolution; in Italy, a bearded Garibaldi in the uniform of the Risorgimento—were typical of the visual reinforcement of appeals to national pride and unity as well as to encourage cohesion with the Allies.

How Effective Were Posters?

No measuring instrument has been devised for a precise evaluation of the effect of posters upon their targets. Evaluations are therefore largely a matter of hunch and of post hoc reasoning—after this, therefore because of it. The war loans were subscribed; ergo, the poster campaigns for them were successful. The Allies won the war; war posters were effective.

The difficulty with this reasoning is that it obviously ignores other factors that contributed to the result. The Axis used posters too, and it lost. According to the post hoc argument, the British poster recruiting campaign in World War I failed because conscription had to be introduced, but it is also possible that the campaign was quite effective within the limits of the potential for psychological persuasion, limits that are unknown.

In the case of war loans, an analogy to the poster campaigns was Kate Smith's singing marathon in World War II, during which millions and millions of dollars were subscribed. What one doesn't know, however, is how much of this money would have been subscribed anyway; or whether some alternative form of massive persuasion would have done as well; or how many of the pledges were repudiated; or how many of the purchased war bonds were quickly resold. In another controversy over alternative means of persuasion, there were many who argued that propaganda leaflets, delivered to the enemy at the risk of men and aircraft, weren't comparable in effectiveness with a well-placed bomb. According to one World War II joke, the first bombs dropped by the British carried a label reading, "You are lucky; this might have been a leaflet."

A conventional view held by students of the subject is that propaganda, including posters, is very successful with those who already believe and useless against those who don't believe, leaving only a small margin of "potential waverers" who may be susceptible to persuasion if given the opportunity and who are in a position to respond. The reply to this view is that—even granting that the effectiveness of propaganda may be marginal—if it shortens a war by even half a day, the savings in lives and money justifies propaganda's relatively small cost. Neither of these views throws any light on the question of the specific effects of the poster.

Common sense suggests that the poster played an important role as simple announcement and publicity—for such things as the need for conservation of fats, the availability of war bonds for purchase, the existence of the war itself—regardless of any persuasive appeal particular posters might or might not have had. This publicity function was particularly important in World War I, when alternative means of communication were absent or were not yet so well developed as they were in the 1940s.

Another value of the poster, more intangible and more difficult to describe, arises from the mere activity of producing it. Just as commercial concerns feel compelled to advertise to enhance their self-image and to prove themselves no less adept than their competitors in utilizing available tools of communication, so governments in time of war feel compelled to prove their propaganda capability to themselves and to show that they are no less adept than their enemies in the exploitation of psychological weaponry. Stated another way, the idea of not using an available propaganda tool, whether of proven effectiveness or not, is scarcely conceivable. Such use is vital to the national leadership for its own self-respect and self-confidence, and employing that tool may therefore be viewed as essential for the successful prosecution of war.

Finally, another intangible value of the poster is the feeling that it is likely to create a sense of involvement in a national mission by providing constant reminders through one image or another that "this is my war, and I am a part of it." Involvement was obviously felt by the many people who planned, produced, and distributed war posters, but it also extended in some degree to everyone within sight of the poster. The beauty of the "careless talk" campaign was that people could feel involved in the war, playing a part in it and combating the enemy, merely by doing nothing and keeping their mouths shut. Similarly, in the more recent case of campaigns to encourage the building of domestic bomb shelters against nuclear attack, the value of building the shelters was not so much real as psychological, creating a consciousness of the threat of an enemy and involving the citizen in an action that made him feel himself to be already enlisted as a participant in an imaginary war.

Poster Collecting

Another value of the poster is retrospective, represented by its attraction for those who collect the images, artifacts, and other mementos of great events in other times. The joys of collecting are not new nor is the phenomenon of poster collecting of recent origin, but the interest of museums as well as of private collectors in the poster, and a rapidly expanding poster literature, suggests both the popularity of poster collecting and a new seriousness of interest. From time to time private collectors convey their posters to research libraries and museums for care and preservation and, as this catalog attests, for the benefit of scholars.

The Marshall Foundation collection owes its existence to the labor or thoughtfulness of a few individuals who had a special awareness of posters and their lasting value. Just as every poster has a history, so does every collection of posters.

The origins of the posters are diverse. For example, a large group of British World War I posters in the Marshall collection was presented to Russell Day Hill of Chicago, when he was in England in 1916 in connection with negotiations for one of the British war loans. When the United States entered the war, Hill applied for a commission, intending to make a patrol boat available to the Navy for antisubmarine duty along the East Coast. In May of 1917, however, he fell victim to the streptococcus epidemic then rampant at the Great Lakes Naval Training Station. The posters passed to his daughter, Helen Hill, later Mrs. Francis Pickens Miller. When Colonel Miller donated his collection of personal papers to the Marshall Foundation, Mrs. Miller included the posters.

Many of the World War II American posters came from the collections of Henry U. Milne, a prodigious collector of Americana for more than fifty years. Milne died in 1967 at age eighty-one. He was said to have had more than 50,000 items in his collections, and on May 28, 1961, *The Sunday Star* reported that he maintained "many, many file cases and packing boxes throughout his house (on Newton Street, N.W., Washington, D.C.) in hallways, the basement and any available spot.

They are bulging with all manner of clippings, papers, murals, special reports, pamphlets, photographs, etchings, prints, and memorabilia of White House personalities." Melvin Ryder of the Army Times Publishing Company acquired the posters when the Milne collections were broken up and subsequently donated them to the Marshall Foundation.

The German posters were literally saved from fiery destruction by Forrest C. Pogue—Marshall biographer and former executive director of the George C. Marshall Research Foundation—when he was an army historian in Germany at the close of World War II. Posters found in barracks and indoctrination schools were ordered burned as propaganda under general regulations, but Pogue was able to save a collection of them, arguing their great historical value. He subsequently donated them to the Marshall Foundation when he became its director.

Posters

The number in parentheses at the end of each legend is the entry number of that poster in the inventory beginning on page 44.

Fig. 1 WW II: United States. (549)

Fig. 2 WW II: United States. (516)

Fig. 3 WW I: United States. (156)

Fig. 4 WW I: France. (11)

Fig. 5 WW I: United States. (574)

Fig. 6 WW II: United States. (602)

Fig. 7 WW I: Great Britain. (72)   *Fig. 8* WW I: France. (35)

Fig. 9 WW I: Great Britain. (88)   *Fig.10* WW I: United States. (168)

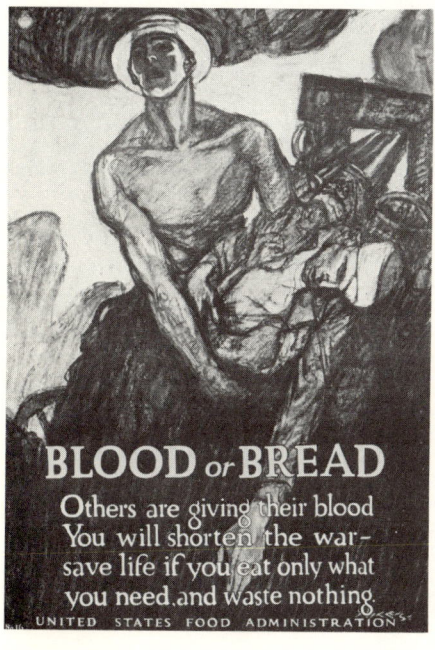 

Fig.11 WW I: United States. (122)   *Fig.12* WW I: France. (15)

Fig.13 WW I: France. (34)   *Fig.14* WWI : United States. (208)

Fig.15 WWI : Great Britain. (108)

Fig.16 WW I: United States. (209)

Fig.17 WW II: United States. (444)

Fig.18 WW II: Germany. (289)

Fig.19 WW I: France. (13)

Fig.20 WW I: France. (14)

Fig.21 WW II: United States. (589)

Fig.22 WW II: United States. (552)

Fig.23 WW I: France. (45)

25

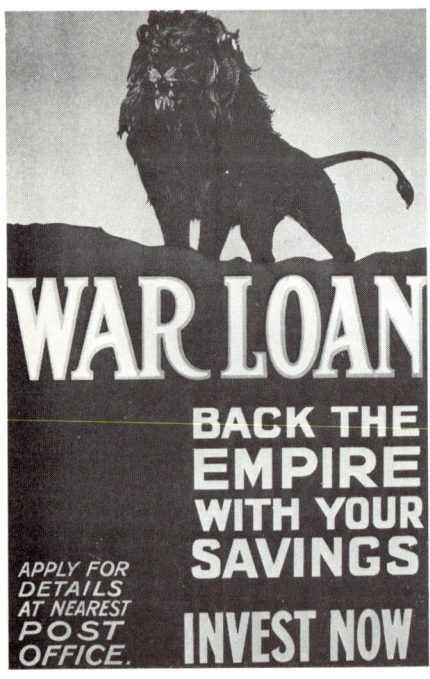
*Fig.*24   WW I: Great Britain. (101)

*Fig.*25   WW II: United States. (535)

*Fig.*26   WW I: United States. (195)

*Fig.*27   WW II: Great Britain. (422)

Fig.28 WW I: France. (20)

Fig.29 WW I: Great Britain. (57)

Fig.30 WW I: United States. (119)

Fig.31 WW I: United States. (198)

Fig.32 WW I: France. (33)

Fig.33 WW I: France. (17)

Fig.34 WW I: France. (42)

Fig.35 WW II: France. (263)

Fig.36 WW I: United States. (169)

Fig.37 WW I: Great Britain. (63)

Fig.38 WW II: Germany. (406)

Fig.39 WW I: France. (25)

Fig.40 WW I: United States. (228)

Fig.41 WW I: France. (19)

Fig.42 WW I: United States. (178)

Fig.43 WW I: United States. (137)   *Fig.44* WW I: United States. (231)

Fig.45 WW I: United States. (189)

Fig. 46 WW II: United States. (498)

Fig.47 WW II: United States. (547)

Fig.48 WW II: United States. (584)

Fig.49 WW II: United States. (646)

Fig.50 WW II: United States. (677)

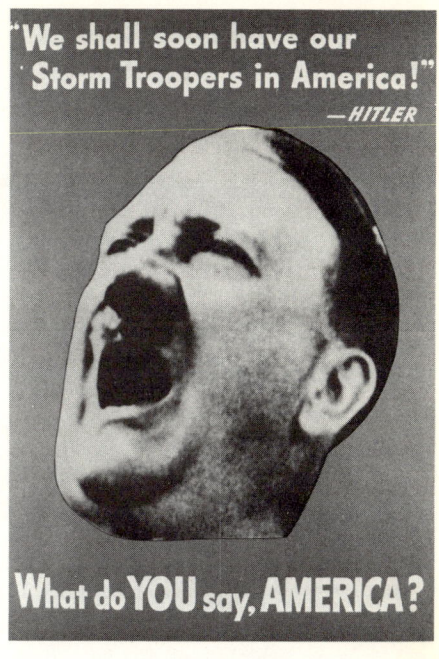

Fig.51 WW II: United States. (668)

Fig.52 WW II: United States. (579)

Fig.53 WW II: United States. (669)

Fig.54 WW II: United States. (572)

Fig.55 WW II: United States. (426)

Fig.56 WW II: United States. (436)

Fig.57 WW II: United States. (465)

Fig.58 WW II: United States. (637)

Fig.59 WW II: Canada. (245)

Fig.60 WW II: Germany(Ukraine).(276)

Fig.61 WW II: Germany. (409)

Fig.62 WW II: Germany. (287)

Fig. 63 WW II: Germany. (275)

Fig.64 WW II: France. (264)

Fig.65 WW II: France. (262)

INVENTORY

INVENTORY

The inventory on the following pages is divided into two major sections: World War I and World War II. The posters are further separated according to country of origin and are then arranged alphabetically by the first word in the top line of the poster legend, except for a series of World War II German "Weekly Slogans of the NSDAP" which is arranged chronologically (entries 289-415).

Provided the information was available, a poster entry contains the following parts:

Accession number. The entries are numbered consecutively 1 through 697. This number corresponds to the accession number of the original poster and to its photograph and slide number.

Legend. The legend is in uppercase letters, with a diagonal line indicating the beginning of each new line on the poster. If the legend is of unusual length, the listing is shortened in the catalog. This is noted by using three periods at the point where the portion of the legend is omitted.

Artist. The name of the artist is given if it appears on the poster or when the artist has been verified from other sources.

Place of the publishing or sponsoring agency and the agency name. The government agency or department which published the poster or had it published is listed, preceded by the location of that agency, when identified on the poster. If only a printing firm and its location are available, they are given. If the poster was part of a specific series, the series number follows the agency name.

Date. A date is listed when printed on the poster.

Color or black and white. Color posters are indicated by "Color"; black and white posters are identified by the abbreviation "B & W."

Size. All sizes are recorded in centimeters, the height followed by the width.

Donors. Donors of posters to the Marshall Foundation are keyed to their donations by the following symbols: Ak, Ian H. Ackroyd-Kelly, deposited in memory of Walter H. Ackroyd-Kelly through the courtesy of the Virginia Military Institute Museum; By, Lelia Cocke Bagbey; Ba, Mrs. M. S. Battle; Bl, George Blow; B, Arthur L. Buck; H, Leigh B. Hanes, Jr. in memory of John D. Guthrie; Mc, Catherine Bemiss

McGuire; M, Helen Hill Miller; PL, Preston Library, Virginia Military Institute; P, Forrest C. Pogue; Re, O. W. Riegel; R, Melvin Ryder; S, Marie Marshall Singer; Sm, Otis D. Smith. Posters acquired by purchase or exchange do not have a symbol at the end of the entry.

Illustration number. The sixty-five posters reproduced in this volume are identified by the figure number in parentheses.

The following is an example of a complete entry:
535. LESS DANGEROUS / THAN CARELESS TALK / DON'T DISCUSS TROOP MOVEMENTS—SHIP SAILINGS—WAR EQUIPMENT. Albert Dorne, artist. Washington: Office of War Information, 1944. Color. 72 x 51. R. (Fig. 25.)

If an entry part could not be determined from the poster or substantiated from another source, it is omitted from the order in that listing.

WORLD WAR I

CANADA

1. BACK THEM UP / MY DUTY / GIVE TO THE / CANADIAN / PATRIOTIC FUND. Hamilton, Ontario: Howell Lith. Co., Ltd. Color. 103 x 69.

2. BRING HIM HOME / WITH THE / VICTORY LOAN. Color. 90 x 61. Mc.

3. DOMINION OF CANADA / VICTORY LOAN / VOTRE / ARGENT! / PLUS / 5½% / D'INTERET / LE CANADA EST VOTRE / GARANTIE / VOYEZ LES JOURNAUX / POR LES DETAILS [. . . Your money plus 5½% interest— Canada is your guarantee—See your newspapers for details]. Color. 90 x 65. Mc.

4. HERE'S YOUR CHANCE / IT'S <u>MEN</u> WE WANT. Toronto: Central Recruiting Committee, no. 2, Military Division. Color. 96 x 63.

5. OH PLEASE / DO! / DADDY / BUY ME A / VICTORY / BOND. Sampson, artist. Color. 90 x 61. Mc.

6. SOUSCRIVEZ A / L'EMPRUNT DE LA "VICTOIRE" [Subscribe to the Victory Loan]. Color. 142 x 101.

FRANCE

7. A LA MEMOIRE DES SOLDATS BELGES MORTS POUR LA PATRIE. / UNION DE FRANCE POUR LA BELGIQUE / ET LES PAYS ALLIES ET AMIS / . . . / EN L'EGLISE DE SAINT SULPICE / LE MARDI 19 DECEMBRE A 4H½. / LA VEILLEE DES TOMBES / CEREMONIE SOLENNELLE / . . . [In memory of the Belgian soldiers who died for their country—The French Union for Belgium and the Allied and Friendly Countries . . . in the Church of St. Sulpice, Tuesday, 19 December at 4:30. The Wake of the Tombs, a solemn ceremony . . .]. Paris: Lapina, 1916. Color. 120 x 80.

8. AH! SI L'ON AVAIT / SUPPRIME / L'ALCOOL / UNION DES FRANCAISES CONTRE L'ALCOOL [Ah! If one could

suppress alcohol—Union of Frenchmen against alcohol]. B. Chavannaz, artist. Paris: Crete. Color. 120 x 80.

9. COMPAGNIE ALGERIENNE / ... / SOUSCRIRE, C'EST HATER SON RETOUR AVEC LA VICTORIE / 3E EMPRUNT DE LA DEFENSE NATIONALE / ... [The Algerian Company ... Subscribe to hasten his return with victory—3rd National Defense Loan ...]. Lucien-Hector Jonas, artist. Paris: Devambez. Color. 120 x 80.

10. COMPAGNIE DES NOTAIRES / DE PARIS & DU DEPARTEMENT DE LA SEINE / FRANCAIS! / SOUSCRIVEZ TOUS / AU 4EME EMPRUNT / DE LA DEFENSE NATIONALE / ON SOUSCRIT SANS FRAIS CHEZ TOUS LES NOTAIRES [Society of Notaries of Paris and of the Department of the Seine—Frenchmen—Subscribe to the 4th National Defense Loan—One can subscribe free of charge at all notaries' offices]. Adolphe Leon Willette, artist. Paris: Devambez, 1916. Color. 120 x 80.

11. COMPTOIR NATIONAL / D'ESCOMPTE DE PARIS / EMPRUNT / NATIONAL / 1918 / POUR HATER LA VICTOIRE / ET POUR NOUS REVOIR BIENTOT, SOUSCRIVEZ! / ON SOUSCRIT SANS FRAIS AU SIEGE SOCIAL, 14, RUE BERGERE, A PARIS / ET DANS TOUTES LES AGENCES OU BUREAUX DE QUARTIER [National Discount Bank of Paris—National Loan of 1918—To hasten the victory and to see us again soon, Subscribe! One can subscribe free of charge at the main office, 14 Rue Bergere, Paris, and at all branch offices or district offices]. Auguste Leroux, artist. Paris: Joseph Charles. Color. 120 x 80. H. (Fig. 4.)

12. CREDIT COMMERCIAL DE FRANCE / 4EME EMPRUNT DE LA DEFENSE NATIONALE—1918 / SOUSCRIVEZ POUR LA VICTOIRE / ET POUR LE TRIOMPHE DE LA LIBERTE [Commercial Credit of France—4th National Defense Loan—1918—Subscribe for victory and for the triumph of liberty]. Lucien-Hector Jonas, artist. Paris: Chacoin, 1918. Color. 119 x 79.

13. CREDIT LYONNAIS / SOUSCRIVES AU 4E EMPRUNT NATIONAL [Lyons Trust—Subscribe to the 4th National Loan]. Jules Abel Faivre, artist. Paris: Devambez. Color. 61 x 80. H. (Fig. 19.)

14. CROIX-ROUGE FRANCAISE / UNION DES FEMMES DE FRANCE / ... / VENTE DE GUERRE / ... [French Red Cross—Union of the Women of France ... War Sale ...]. Georges Dorival and Georges Capon, artists. Paris: Dorival, 1916. Color. 120 x 80. (Fig. 20.)

15. 12 SEPTEMBRE / 1915 / JOURNEE / DE / L'OEUVRE NIVERNAISE / DES / MUTILES DE LA GUERRE [12 September 1915—Day of the work of the Nivernaise women for the disabled war veterans. Maurice Neumont, artist. Paris: Devambez, 1915. Color. 115 x 79. (Fig. 12.)

16. EMPRUNT DE LA DEFENSE NATIONALE / N'OUBLIE PAS DE SOUSCRIRE ... POUR / LA VICTOIRE! ... ET LE RETOUR! / ... [National Defense Loan—do not forget to subscribe—for victory and the reunion ...]. Francisque Poulbot, artist. Paris: Devambez, 1915. Color. 110 x 77.

17. EMPRUNT DE LA LIBERATION / ON / LES / A / SOUSCRIVEZ A LA / LONDON COUNTY & WESTMINSTER BANK (PARIS) LTD. / 22, PLACE VENDOME—PARIS [Loan of the Liberation—We have them—Subscribe at the London County & Westminster Bank (Paris), Ltd.—22 Place Vendome—Paris]. Firmen Boursset, artist. Paris: Vaugirard. Color. 120 x 80. H. (Fig. 33.)

18. EMPRUNT DE LA LIBERATION / ON SOUSCRIT A LA / BANQUE D'ALSACE ET DE LORRAINE / ... [Loan of the Liberation—Subscribe at the Bank of Alsace and Lorraine ...]. Hansi [Jean Jacques Waltz], artist. Paris: Lapina, 1917. Color. 80 x 60. Ba.

19. EMPRUNT / DEFENSE NATIONALE / —EUX AUSSI! / FONT LEUR DEVOIR / PUBLIE SOUS LES AUSPICES DE L'UNION DES SOCIETES DE TIR DE FRANCE / ET DE L'UNION DES SOCIETES DE GYMNASTIQUE DE FRANCE [National Defense Loan—They also! Do their duty—Published under the auspices of the Union of Shooting Societies of France and the Union of Gymnastic Societies of France]. Jules Adler, artist. Paris: Crete. Color. 120 x 80. (Fig. 41.)

20. EMPRUNT NATIONAL 1918 / SOCIETE / GENERALE / POUR NOUS RENDRE / ENTIERE / LA DOUCE TERRE

DE FRANCE [National Loan 1918—Societe Generale—so we can make whole the sweet land of France]. B. Chavannaz, artist. Paris: Crete. Color. 80 x 120. (Fig. 28.)

21. GRAND SALLE DU TROCADERO—DIMANCHE 3 DECEMBRE 1916 A 2H PRECISES / FEDERATION MUTUALISTE DE LA SEINE / ... / MATINEE POPULAIRE EXTRAORDINAIRE / AU PROFIT DES / ORPHELINS MUTUALISTES DE LA GUERRE / ... [Grand Hall of the Trocadero—Sunday 3 December 1916 at precisely 2 o'clock—Mutual Federation of the Seine ... an extraordinary people's matinee for the benefit of the War Orphans' Mutual Benefit Society ...]. Louis Flot, artist. Paris: Devambez, 1916. Color. 83 x 73.

22. JOURNEE DE L'ARMEE D'AFRIQUE / ET DES TROUPES COLONIALES [African Army and Colonial Troops Day]. Lucien-Hector Jonas, artist. Paris: Devambez. Color. 121 x 80. Ba.

23. JOURNEE DE PARIS / 14 JUILLET / 1915 / AU PROFIT DES / OEUVRES DE GUERRE / DE L'HOTEL-DE-VILLE / POUR LES COMBATTANTS / LES BLESSES / LES CONVALESCENTS / LES MUTILES / LES REFUGIES / LES PRISONNIERS [Paris Day—14 July 1915—for the benefit of the war works of the Hotel-de-Ville—for the fighting men, the wounded, the convalescents, the maimed, the refugees, the prisoners]. G. Picard, artist. Paris: Devambez, 1915. Color. 119 x 79.

24. JOURNEE DU POILU / POUR QUE PAPA VIENNE EN PERMISSION, S'IL VOUS PLAIT, / 25 ET 26 / DECEMBRE / 1915 / ORGANISEE PAR LE PARLEMENT [Infantrymen's Day—so papa can come home on leave, please—25 and 26 December 1915—organized by the Parlement]. Francisque Poulbot, artist. Paris: Devambez, 1915. Color. 120 x 80.

25. JOURNEE DU POILU / 25 ET 26 / DECEMBRE / 1915 / ORGANISEE PAR LE PARLEMENT [Infantrymen's Day—25 and 26 December 1915—organized by the Parlement]. Maurice Neumont, artist. Paris: Devambez, 1915. Color. 120 x 80. H. (Fig. 39.)

WW I: FRANCE

26. JOURNEE NATIONALE / DES ORPHELINS—GUERRE 1914-15-16 / PETITS FRANCAIS ET PETITES FRANCAISES, POUR LES / ENFANTS DONT LES PAPAS NE SONT PLUS, DONNEZ CE QUE / VOUS POUVEZ, DONNEZ UN PEU DE VOTRE JOIE, DONNEZ / UN PEU DE VOTRE BIEN . . . / . . . / LES DONS ET SOUSCRIPTIONS DOIVENT ETRE ADRESSES AU SIEGE SOCIAL DU COMITE-33 RUE BONAPARTE. VI; PARIS [National Orphans' Day—the War of 1914-15-16—Little French boys and girls—for the children whose fathers are no more, give what you can, give a little of your joy, give a little of your comfort . . . Gifts and subscriptions should be addressed to the main office of the Committee, 33 Rue Bonaparte. VI; Paris]. Bernard Naudin, artist. Paris: "Le Papier," 1916. Color. 120 x 81.

27. JOURNEE SERBE / 25 JUIN / 1916 [Serbian Day, 25 June 1916]. Mourgue, artist. Paris: Chambrellent, 1916. Color. 80 x 120.

28. L'EMPRUNT DE LA LIBERATION [The Loan of the Liberation]. Jules Abel Faivre, artist. Paris: Pichot. Color. 80 x 113. Ba.

29. L'INFANTERIE / FRANCAISE / DANS LA BATAILLE [The French Infantry in battle]. H. Delaspre, artist. Paris: Jouchet-Publicite. Color. 120 x 80. Ba.

30. LA JOURNEE / DU POILU / 25 DECEMBRE / 26 DECEMBRE / 1915 / LE POILU / AVEC VOUS ET / PAR VOUS NOUS / JURONS DE SAUVER / LA FRANCE / LEON GAMBLETTE [Infantrymen's Day—25 December—26 December 1915—The infantryman—with you and through you we vow to save France—Leon Gamblette]. Lucien-Hector Jonas, artist. Paris: I. Lapina, 1915. Color. 120 x 80.

31. LA VOLONTE D'AGRESSION / DE L'ALLEMAGNE / EST ETABLIE / PAR L'ACCUMULATION SECRETE D'UN MATERIEL DE GUERRE / . . .[Germany's aggressive will is established by its secret accumulation of war materials so disproportionate to that of the neighboring peoples whose purpose is simply defense. July 1914-the two sides of the frontier . . .]. Paris: Typographie Ad Marechal. Color. 68 x 48. Ak.

32. OFFICE CENTRAL DES OEUVRES DE BIENFAISANCE / . . . / EXPOSITION-VENTE / DE TABLEAUX / OFFERTS PAR LES ARTISTES / AU PROFIT DE LA SECTION DU / PRET D'HONNEUR / AUX AVEUGLES / DE LA GUERRE / . . . [Central Office of Charitable Works . . . Exhibition-Sale of paintings given by the artists to benefit the section of the honor pay devoted to those blinded by war . . .]. Theophile-Alexandre Steinlen, artist. Paris: Editions "La Guerre," 1917. Color. 80 x 113.

33. ON LES AURA! / 2E EMPRUNT / DE / LA DEFENSE NATIONALE / SOUSCRIVEZ [We will get them--2nd National Defense Loan--Subscribe]. Jules Abel Faivre, artist. Paris: Devambez, 1916. Color. 104 x 79. H. (Fig. 32.)

34. ON NE PASSE PAS! / 1914 1918 / PAR DEUX FOIS J'AI TENU ET VAINCU SUR LA MARNE, / CIVIL, MON FRERE, / LA SOURNOISE OFFENSIVE DE LA "PAIX BLANCHE" VA T'ASSAILLIR A TON TOUR, / COMME MOI, TU DOIS TENIR ET VAINCRE, SOIS FORT ET MALIN. / MEFIE-TOI DE L'HYPOCRISIE BOCHE [They shall not pass! 1914-1918—Twice I have stood fast and conquered on the Marne, civilian, my brother—A false "peace offensive" will attack you in turn—Like me, you must stand firm and conquer, be strong and shrewd. Beware of Boche hypocrisy.]. Maurice Neumont, artist. Paris: Grandes Associations Francaises contre la Propagande Ennemie, 1918. Color. 113 x 76. R. (Fig. 13.)

35. POUR LA FRANCE / VERSEZ VOTRE OR / L'OR COMBAT POUR LA VICTOIRE [For France, pour out your gold—gold fights for victory]. Jules Abel Faivre, artist. Paris: Devambez. Color. 120 x 80. (Fig. 8.)

36. POUR LE SUPREME EFFORT / EMPRUNT NATIONAL / SOCIETE GENERALE [For the supreme effort—National Loan—Societe Generale]. M. Falter and Atetien Pichon, artists. Paris: Chaix. Color. 109 x 80.

37. POUR QUE VOS ENFANTS NE CONNAISSENT PLUS / LES HORREURS DE LA GUERRE, / SOUSCRIVEZ / A L'EMPRUNT NATIONAL / SOCIETE GENERALE [So your children will not have to know the horrors of war, subscribe to the National Loan—Societe Generale]. Georges Reson, artist. Paris: Devambez, 1917. Color. 80 x 56. H.

38. 14 JUILLET 1916 / JOURNEE DE PARIS / AU PROFIT DES OEUVRES DE GUERRE / DE L'HOTEL DE VILLE [14 July 1916—Paris Day—for the benefit of the war works of the Hotel-de-Ville]. Francisque Poulbot, artist. Paris: H. Chacoin, 1916. Color. 120 x 80.

39. REPUBLIQUE FRANCAISE / 3E EMPRUNT DE LA DEFENSE / NATIONALE [French Republic—3rd National Defense Loan]. A. LeLong, artist. Paris: Draeger. Color. 81 x 120. Ba.

40. Same as 39. H.

41. SOLDAT, / LA PATRIE COMPTE / SUR TOI: GARDE / LUI TOUTES TES / FORCES / RESISTE AUX / SEDUCTIONS DE LA / RUE OU TE GUETTE / LA MALADIE AUSSI / DANGEREUSE QUE / LA GUERRE / ELLE CONDUIT SES / VICTIMES A LA / DECHEANCE ET / A LA MORT SANS / UTILITE, SANS / HONNEUR [Soldier, our country is counting on you; save all your strength for her. Resist the seductions of the path toward illness, which lies in wait for you, and is as dangerous as war itself. It guides its victims to disgrace and to a useless death, without honor.] Theophile-Alexandre Steinlen, artist. Paris: Lith. Berger-Leurault, 1918. Color. 80 x 60. Ak.

42. SOUSCRIVEZ POUR LA VICTOIRE / BANQUE NATIONALE DE CREDIT [Subscribe for Victory—National Trust Bank]. M. Richard Outz, artist. Paris: Devambez, 1916. Color. 80 x 120. Ba. (Fig. 34.)

43. 3E EMPRUNT / DE LA DEFENSE NATIONALE / CREDIT LYONNAIS / SOUSCRIVEZ [3rd National Defense Loan—Lyons Trust—Subscribe]. Jules Abel Faivre, artist. Paris: Devambez. Color. 79 x 57. H.

44. 3E EMPRUNT / DE LA DEFENSE NATIONALE / SOUSCRIVEZ / POUR LA FRANCE QUI COMBAT! / POUR CELLE QUI CHAQUE JOUR GRANDIT [3rd National Defense Loan—Subscribe for the France that fights! For those who grow taller each day]. Auguste Leroux, artist. Paris: Joseph Charles. Color. 114 x 80. H.

45. UN / DERNIER / EFFORT / ET ON / L'AURA [One last effort and we will beat them]. Courboin, artist. Paris: Cornille & Serre. Color. 120 x 80. (Fig. 23.)

46. UNION DES FAMILLES FRANCAISES ET ALLIEES / . . . / AIDE AUX MERES VEUVES ET ORPHELINS / DES SOLDATS MORTS AU CHAMP D'HONNEUR / FRERES ET SOEURS DE GUERRE [Union of French and Allied Families . . . Help widowed mothers and orphans of the soldiers dead on the field of honor—brothers and sisters of war]. Germaine Lavaire, artist. Paris: Devambez. Color. 106 x 73.

47. VIVE LA NATION! [Long live the nation!] Adolphe Leon Willette, artist. Paris: Devambez, 1917. Color. 120 x 81.

48. VOUS AUSSI FAITES VOTRE DEVOIR: / AVEC TOUTES VOS RESSOURCES / SOUSCRIVEZ A L'EMPRUNT / CREDIT COMMERCIAL DE FRANCE [You also do your duty: with all your resources subscribe to the Loan of the Commercial Credit of France]. B. Chavannaz, artist. Paris: Crete. Color. 119 x 80. H.

GREAT BRITAIN

49. APPEAL TO WOMEN / MAKE EVERY / PENNY DO THE / WORK OF TWO / PUT YOUR SAVINGS / IN THE / WAR LOAN. London: The Parliamentary War Savings Committee, no. 3, 1915. Color. 76 x 51. M.

50. ARE YOU IN THIS? Lt. Gen. Sir. R.S.S. Baden Powell, artist. London: The Parliamentary Recruiting Committee, no. 112. Color. 76 x 50. M.

51. BACK THEM UP / MY DUTY / INVEST IN THE / WAR LOAN. E. V. Kealey, artist. London: The Parliamentary War Savings Committee, no. 15, 1915. Color. 75 x 51. M.

52. "BE HONEST WITH / YOURSELF. BE CERTAIN / THAT YOUR SO-CALLED / REASON IS NOT A / SELFISH EXCUSE" / LORD KITCHENER / ENLIST TO-DAY. V. Soutary, artist. London: The Parliamentary Recruiting Committee, no. 127. Color. 76 x 51. M.

53. BRITISHERS / ENLIST TO-DAY / 280 BROADWAY. Guy Lipscombe, artist. New York: The Hegeman Printing Co. Color. 100 x 68. Ak.

54. BRITISHERS / YOU'RE NEEDED / COME ACROSS NOW. Lloyd Meyers, artist. New York: British & Canadian Recruiting Mission. Color. 105 x 71. Ak.

55. BUY WAR LOAN / . . . / AND YOU WILL HELP / YOUR COUNTRY AND / OUR BRAVE TROOPS / IN THE FIGHTING LINE. London: The Parliamentary War Savings Committee, no. 14. Color. 75 x 51. M.

56. DO YOU THINK / MY 5/- WON'T HELP THE WAR LOAN / DO YOU REALIZE / THOUSANDS MAY BE THINKING THE SAME / DO YOU KNOW / IF EACH OF US SAVED 5/- A WEEK / WE SHOULD SAVE NEARLY / £600,000,000 A YEAR / INVEST YOUR 5/- TO-DAY / APPLY AT THE NEAREST POST OFFICE. London: The Parliamentary War Savings Committee, no. 20. Color. 76 x 51. M.

57. 1805 "ENGLAND EXPECTS" 1915 / ARE YOU DOING YOUR DUTY TO-DAY? London: The Parliamentary Recruiting Committee, no. 101. Color. 49 x 84. M. (Fig. 29.)

58. ENLIST TO-DAY. / HE'S / HAPPY & / SATISFIED / ARE YOU? London: The Parliamentary Recruiting Committee, no. 96. Color. 76 x 51. M.

59. EVERYONE / SHOULD DO HIS BIT / ENLIST NOW. Baron Low, artist. London: The Parliamentary Recruiting Committee, no. 121, 1915. Color. 74 x 50. M.

60. Same as 59. Ak.

61. FALL IN / ANSWER NOW / IN YOUR COUNTRY'S / HOUR OF NEED. E.V. Kealey, artist. London: The Parliamentary Recruiting Committee, no. 12. Color. 73 x 49. Ak.

62. FOLLOW ME! / YOUR COUNTRY / NEEDS YOU. E.V. Kealey, artist. London: The Parliamentary Recruiting Committee, no. 11. Color. 73 x 49. Ak.

63. FORWARD! / FORWARD TO VICTORY / ENLIST NOW. Lucy Elizabeth Kemp-Welsh, artist. London: The Parliamen-

tary Recruiting Committee, no. 133, 1915. Color. 76 x 49. M. (Fig. 37.)

64. Same as 63. Ak.

65. HELP YOUR COUNTRY / INVEST / 5/- / TO-DAY / IN THE / WAR LOAN / APPLY AT NEAREST POST OFFICE. London: The Parliamentary War Savings Committee, no. 4. Color. 77 x 51. M.

66. IF YOU BUY THE / NEW WAR LOAN / YOUR COUNTRY GETS / FUNDS TO CARRY ON / AND WIN THE WAR / YOU GET / 4'6 A YEAR FOR EVERY / Ł5 OF LOAN YOU BUY / WITH AN INVESTMENT / GUARANTEED BY THE STATE / INFORMATION AT ANY POST OFFICE. London: The Parliamentary War Savings Committee, no. 7, 1915. Color. 76 x 51. M.

67. IS YOUR HOME HERE? / DEFEND IT! / RECRUITING GROUNDS OF THE REGULAR ARMY / ... / RECRUITING GROUNDS OF THE TERRITORIAL FORCE / . . . . London: The Parliamentary Recruiting Committee, no. 126. Color. 95 x 62. M.

68. IT IS GOING TO BE A LONG / DRAWN-OUT STRUGGLE. / WE SHALL NOT SHEATHE / THE SWORD UNTIL . . . / . . . / THE PRIME MINISTER / AT THE GUILDHALL / NOVEMBER 9TH, 1914. London: The Parliamentary Recruiting Committee, no. 110. Color. 76 x 51. M.

69. IT'S OUR FLAG / FIGHT FOR IT / WORK FOR IT. Guy Lipscombe, artist. London: The Parliamentary Recruiting Committee, no. 107, 1915. Color. 151 x 99. M.

70. JOIN THE BRAVE THRONG THAT GOES MARCHING ALONG. Gerald Good, artist. London: The Parliamentary Recruiting Committee, no. 118. Color. 16 x 74. M.

71. JOIN THE ROYAL / MARINES / HELP TO MAN THE / GUNS OF THE FLEET / APPLY TO / . . . London: Admiralty Recruiting Department. Color. 76 x 51. Ak.

72. LEND YOUR / FIVE SHILLINGS / TO YOUR COUNTRY / AND / CRUSH / THE GERMANS. D. D. Foy, artist. London: The Parliamentary War Savings Committee, no. 23, 1915. Color. 76 x 51. M. (Fig. 7.)

73. LORD KITCHENER / SAYS:—'MEN, MATERIALS & MONEY / ARE THE IMMEDIATE / NECESSITIES / DOES THE CALL OF DUTY / FIND NO RESPONSE IN YOU / UNTIL REINFORCED— / LET US RATHER SAY / SUPERSEDED— / BY THE CALL OF / COMPULSION?' / LORD KITCHENER SPEAKING AT GUILDHALL JULY 9TH 1915 / ENLIST TO-DAY. Bassano Ltd., artist. London: The Parliamentary Recruiting Committee, no. 113, 1915. Color. 40 x 76. M.

74. LORD KITCHENER / SAYS:— / 'MEN, MATERIALS & MONEY / ARE THE IMMEDIATE / NECESSITIES / DOES THE CALL OF DUTY / FIND NO RESPONSE IN YOU / UNTIL REINFORCED— / LET US RATHER SAY / SUPERSEDED— / BY THE CALL OF / COMPULSION?' / LORD KITCHENER SPEAKING AT GUILDHALL, JULY 9TH 1915 / ENLIST TO-DAY. Bassano Ltd., artist. London: The Parliamentary Recruiting Committee, no. 117, 1915. Color. 102 x 126. M.

75. MAKE US AS PROUD OF YOU / AS WE ARE OF HIM! London: The Parliamentary Recruiting Committee, no. 119, 1915. Color. 76 x 51. M.

76. NEW LANDLORDS FOR OLD. London: Waterlow Bros. & Layton Ltd. Color. 51 x 76. Ak.

77. PAY YOUR / 5/- / FOR / THIS / AND HELP / CRUSH THE GERMANS / APPLY AT THE NEAREST POST OFFICE. London: The Parliamentary War Savings Committee, no. 1, 1915. Color. 76 x 50. M.

78. REMEMBER THE LUSITANIA! / ONE MOTHER LOST ALL HER THREE YOUNG / . . . / ENLIST TO-DAY. London: The Parliamentary Recruiting Committee, no. 95. Color. 102 x 128. M.

79. SPEED THE / "SILVER BULLET" / BUY / THE NEW / GOVERNMENT / WAR LOAN— / 4½ PER CENT PER ANNUM. London: The Parliamentary War Savings Committee, no. 3. Color. 102 x 64. M.

80. STEP INTO YOUR PLACE. London: The Parliamentary Recruiting Committee, no. 104, 1915. Color. 51 x 76. M.

WW I: GREAT BRITAIN

81. Same as 80. Ak.

82. SURELY YOU WILL / FIGHT FOR YOUR / [picture of George V] / AND / [map of British Isles] / COME ALONG, BOYS, / BEFORE IT IS TOO LATE. London: The Parliamentary Recruiting Committee, no. 83. Color. 74 x 50. M.

83. TAKE UP THE / SWORD OF JUSTICE. Bernard Parkridge, artist. London: The Parliamentary Recruiting Committee, no. 105, 1915. Color. 63 x 102. M.

84. Same as 83. The Parliamentary Recruiting Committee, no. 111. 74 x 51. Ak.

85. Same as 84. 36 x 51. M.

86. TAKE UP THE SWORD OF / JUSTICE / JOIN NOW. London: The Parliamentary Recruiting Committee, no. 123, 1915. Color. 18 x 76. Ak.

87. Same as 86. 15 x 76. M.

88. THE BRITISH / SOVEREIGN / WILL WIN / INVEST / IN THE / WAR LOAN / TO-DAY / ASK FOR DETAILS AT NEAREST POST OFFICE. London: The Parliamentary War Savings Committee, no. 9, 1915. Color. 76 x 50. M. (Fig. 9.)

89. Same as 88. Ak.

90. THE KEY TO THE / SITUATION / MUNITIONS / MEN / AND / MONEY / ARE / YOU / HELPING / TO / TURN IT? London: The Parliamentary Recruiting Committee, no. 116. Color. 74 x 49. M.

91. THE LIFE-LINE IS FIRM / THANKS TO THE / MERCHANT NAVY. Charles Wood, artist. London: H.M.S.O. Color. 75 x 50. Ak.

92. THE NAVY / WANTS / MEN / APPLY TO / . . . London: Admiralty Recruiting Department. Color. 76 x 51. Ak.

93. THE / SCRAP OF PAPER / PRUSSIA'S PERFIDY—BRITAIN'S BOND. / . . . / ENLIST TO-DAY. London: The Parliamentary Recruiting Committee, no. 7. Color. 76 x 52. Ak.

94. THE "SCRAP OF PAPER" / ... / THESE ARE THE SIGNATURES AND SEALS OF THE REPRESENTATIVES / ... / ENLIST TO-DAY. London: Parliamentary Recruiting Committee, no. 15. Color. 73 x 48. VMI.

95. THERE ARE / THREE / TYPES OF MEN / THOSE WHO HEAR / THE CALL AND OBEY / THOSE WHO DELAY / AND—THE OTHERS / TO WHICH DO / YOU BELONG? London: The Parliamentary Recruiting Committee, no. 103. Color. 74 x 50. M.

96. THERE'S ROOM / FOR YOU / ENLIST / TO-DAY. W.A. Fry, artist. London: The Parliamentary Recruiting Committee, no. 122. Color. 78 x 51. M.

97. Same as 96. Ak.

98. TURN YOUR SILVER / INTO BULLETS / AT THE / POST / OFFICE. London: The Parliamentary War Savings Committee, no. 19. Color. 77 x 51. M.

99. WANTED / MEN / MUNITIONS / MONEY / —IF YOU CAN NEITHER ENLIST / NOR MAKE MUNITIONS— / BUY / THE NEW / 4½% / WAR LOAN! Paxter, artist. London: The Parliamentary War Savings Committee, no. 13. Color. 75 x 50. M.

100. Same as 99. Ak.

101. WAR LOAN / BACK THE / EMPIRE / WITH YOUR / SAVINGS / INVEST NOW / APPLY FOR / DETAILS / AT NEAREST / POST / OFFICE. London: The Parliamentary War Savings Committee, no. 21. Color. 76 x 51. M. (Fig. 24.)

102. WAR LOAN / INVEST / FIVE SHILLINGS / AND HELP YOUR COUNTRY / TO WIN / APPLY FOR DETAILS AT THE NEAREST POST OFFICE. London: The Parliamentary War Savings Committee, no. 2. Color. 76 x 51. M.

103. Same as 102. Ak.

104. WAR / LOAN / INVEST TO-DAY / APPLY AT NEAREST POST OFFICE. London: The Parliamentary War Savings Committee, no. 10. Color. 76 x 51. M.

105. WAR LOAN / LEND YOUR SAVINGS / TO THE NATION / TO-DAY / APPLY FOR PARTICULARS AT THE

NEAREST POST OFFICE. London: The Parliamentary War Savings Committee, no. 22. Color. 76 x 51. M.

106. WAR LOAN / "THE MAN, BE HE RICH / OR POOR, IS LITTLE / TO BE ENVIED WHO / AT THIS SUPREME / MOMENT FAILS TO / BRING FORWARD HIS / SAVINGS FOR THE / SECURITY OF HIS / COUNTRY." / THE CHANCELLOR OF THE EXCHEQUER. London: The Parliamentary War Savings Committee, no. 17. Color. 74 x 50. M.

107. WHICH? / HAVE YOU A REASON— / OR ONLY AN / EXCUSE— / FOR NOT ENLISTING / NOW! London: The Parliamentary Recruiting Committee, no. 128. Color. 76 x 50. M.

108. WHO'S ABSENT? / IS IT YOU? London: The Parliamentary Recruiting Committee, no. 125. Color. 74 x 51. M. (Fig. 15.)

109. YOU CAN HELP / TO WIN THE WAR / WITH 5/- / A / SAFE AND PATRIOTIC / INVESTMENT / APPLY AT THE NEAREST POST OFFICE. London: The Parliamentary War Savings Committee, no. 12, 1915. Color. 74 x 49. M.

110. YOU HAVE IN YOUR / POCKET / SILVER BULLETS / THAT WILL STOP THE / GERMANS / LEND THEM TO YOUR COUNTRY / BY / INVESTING IN THE WAR LOAN / TO-DAY. London: The Parliamentary War Savings Committee, no. 6, 1915. Color. 77 x 51. M.

111. YOU HAVE IN / YOUR POCKET / SILVER BULLETS / THAT WILL STOP / THE GERMANS / LEND THEM TO / YOUR COUNTRY / BY / INVESTING IN THE / WAR LOAN / TO-DAY. London: The Parliamentary War Savings Committee, no. 8, 1915. Color. 74 x 48. M.

112. Same as 111. Ak.

113. YOUR KING & COUNTRY / NEED YOU / A WEE "SCRAP O' PAPER" IS BRITAIN'S BOND / TO MAINTAIN THE HONOUR AND GLORY / OF THE / BRITISH EMPIRE. Lawson Wood, artist. London: The Parliamentary Recruiting Committee, no. 17, 1914. Color. 74 x 50. Ak.

59

UNITED STATES

114. "AMMUNITION!" / AND REMEMBER— / BONDS BUY BULLETS! V. Lynch, artist. Philadelphia: Ketterlinus, 1918. Color. 76 x 51.

115. ARE YOU 100% / AMERICAN? / PROVE IT! / BUY / U.S. GOVERNMENT BONDS / THIRD LIBERTY LOAN / . . . Stern, artist. New York: Sackett & Wilhelms Corp. Color. 77 x 51. PL.

116. ARE YOU 100% / AMERICAN? / PROVE IT! / BUY / U.S. GOVERNMENT BONDS / THIRD / LIBERTY LOAN. Stern, artist. New York: Sackett & Wilhelms Corp. Color. 77 x 51. Ak.

117. ARE YOU WORKING / WITH SCHWAB? / CHARLES M. SCHWAB / DIRECTOR GENERAL OF THE EMERGENCY FLEET CORPORATION / SAYS / . . . Philadelphia: Emergency Fleet Corporation. Color. 81 x 55.

118. BE PATRIOTIC / SIGN YOUR COUNTRY'S / PLEDGE TO SAVE THE FOOD. Paul Stahr, artist. New York: U. S. Food Administration. Color. 74 x 54. Ak.

119. BEAT BACK THE HUN / WITH / LIBERTY / BONDS. F. Strothmann, artist. Color. 76 x 51. Mc. (Fig. 30.)

120. Same as 119. Ak.

121. BENEFIT / UNITED WAR WORK FUND / TEAMS OF THE HARVARD RADIOS VS. / PRINCETON AVIATORS / NOV. 23RD AT POLO GROUNDS / TICKETS FOR SALE AT ALL TICKET AGENCIES / UNITED WAR WORK CAMPAIGN / 7. Liello, artist. Color. 67 x 49.

122. BLOOD OR BREAD / OTHERS ARE GIVING THEIR BLOOD / YOU WILL SHORTEN THE WAR—/ SAVE LIFE IF YOU EAT ONLY WHAT / YOU NEED, AND WASTE NOTHING. / UNITED STATES FOOD ADMINISTRATION. Boston: Forbes. Color. 74 x 51. (Fig. 11.)

123. BRITAIN'S DAY / DECEMBER 7 / 1918 / AMERICA'S TRIBUTE TO BRITAIN FOR HER PART IN THE WORLD WAR / MASS MEETING—HIPPODROME— SUNDAY 3 P.M. DECEMBER 7. Color. 97 x 67.

124. BUY / LIBERTY BONDS / "THAT GOVERNMENT OF / THE PEOPLE, BY THE PEOPLE, / FOR THE PEOPLE SHALL NOT / PERISH FROM THE EARTH" / A. LINCOLN. New York: American Lithograph Co. Color. 77 x 51. PL.

125. BUY UNITED STATES GOVERNMENT / WAR SAVINGS STAMPS / YOUR MONEY BACK WITH INTEREST FROM THE UNITED STATES TREASURY. New York: U. S. Treasury Department. Color. 76 x 101. Ak.

126. CAN / VEGETABLES / FRUIT AND / THE KAISER TOO / WRITE FOR FREE BOOK TO / NATIONAL WAR GARDEN COMMISSION / WASHINGTON, D.C. J. Paul Verrees, artist. Washington: National War Garden Commission, 1918. Color. 53 x 36. Ak.

127. CANTIGNY / CHATEAU THIERRY / ST. MIHIEL / ARGONNE / MARNE / "PUT FIGHTING BLOOD IN YOUR BUSINESS HERE'S HIS RECORD! DOES HE GET A JOB?" / —ARTHUR WOODS, ASSISTANT TO THE SECRETARY OF WAR / LIST YOUR EMPLOYMENT NEEDS WITH THE U. S. EMPLOYMENT SERVICE / ... Dan Smith, artist. Baltimore: Thomsen-Ellis Co. Color. 49 x 72. PL.

128. CLEAR—THE—WAY—!! / BUY BONDS / FOURTH / LIBERTY LOAN. Howard Chandler Christy, artist. Boston: Forbes. Color. 76 x 51. Mc.

129. COLORED MAN IS NO SLACKER. Chicago: E. G. Renesch, 1918. Color. 51 x 40. PL.

130. COLUMBIA / CALLS / ENLIST / NOW / FOR / U. S. / ARMY / NEAREST RECRUITING STATION / ... New York: 1916. Color. 101 x 76. Ak.

131. COME / ON! / BUY MORE / LIBERTY BONDS. Walter Whitehead, artist. Philadelphia: Ketterlinus, 1918. Color. 76 x 50.

132. CRUSH THE PRUSSIAN / BUY A BOND / 3RD LIBERTY LOAN. Color. 106 x 71. Ak.

133. DECEMBER 16TH TO 23RD / WHERE / COLUMBIA / SETS / HER NAME / LET / EVERY ONE / OF YOU /

FOLLOW / HER / RED CROSS / CHRISTMAS ROLL CALL. E. H. Blashfield, artist. 1918. Color. 71 x 46. Mc.

134. Same as 133. Ak.

135. ENLIST IN THE NAVY / AMERICANS! / STAND BY / UNCLE SAM FOR / LIBERTY AGAINST / TYRANNY! / THEODORE ROOSEVELT. Louis Raemaekers, artist. New York: U. S. Navy Publicity Bureau. Color. 71 x 86. Ak.

136. ENLIST IN THE NAVY / TO ARMS / U. S. NAVY RECRUITING STATION. Milton Bancroft, artist. Color. 105 x 69. Ak.

137. FIGHT / OR / BUY BONDS / THIRD / LIBERTY LOAN. Howard Chandler Christy, artist. Boston: Forbes, 1917. Color. 102 x 71. Mc. (Fig. 43.)

138. Same as 137. 76 x 51. PL.

139. Same as 137. 76 x 51. Ak.

140. FIGHT WORLD FAMINE / ENROLL IN / THE BOYS' WORKING RESERVE. Baltimore: U. S. Employment Service, Department of Labor. Color. 71 x 48.

141. FOLLOW THE BOYS IN BLUE / FOR HOME AND COUNTRY / ENLIST IN THE NAVY. George Wright, artist. New York: U. S. Navy Publicity Bureau. Color. 50 x 73.

142. Same as 141. 59 x 74. Ak.

143. FOOD IS / AMMUNITION— / DON'T WASTE IT. J.F. Sheridan, artist. U.S. Food Administration. Color. 74 x 53. Ak.

144. FOR HOME AND COUNTRY / VICTORY LIBERTY LOAN. Alfred Everitt Orr, artist. New York: American Lithographic Co., 1918. Color. 102 x 77. PL.

145. FOR VICTORY, BUY MORE BONDS / FOURTH LIBERTY LOAN. J. Scott Williams, artist. Color. 93 x 139. Ak.

146. "GOOD BYE, DAD, I'M OFF / TO FIGHT FOR OLD GLORY, / YOU BUY U. S. GOV'T / BONDS" / THIRD LIBERTY LOAN. Laurence S. Harris, artist. New York: Sackett & Wilhelms Corp. Color. 75 x 51. PL.

147. HALT THE HUN / BUY U. S. GOVERNMENT BONDS / THIRD LIBERTY LOAN. Henry Patrick Raleigh, artist. Chicago: Edwards & Deutsch Litho. Co. Color. 76 x 51. R.

148. HAVE YOU A / RED CROSS SERVICE FLAG? / 1918. Jessie Willcox Smith, artist. Boston: Forbes, 1918. Color. 71 x 51. Mc.

149. Same as 148. Ak.

150. HAVE YOU ANSWERED THE RED CROSS / CHRISTMAS ROLL CALL? Harrison C. Fisher, artist. American National Red Cross, 1918. Color. 76 x 57. Mc.

151. Same as 150. Ak.

152. HAY / ENRIGHT / GRESHAM / "THE FIRST THREE!" / GIVE TILL IT HURTS / —THEY GAVE TILL THEY / DIED / WAR FUND WEEK ONE HUNDRED MILLION DOLLARS. Kidder, artist. Color. 70 x 57. Ak.

153. HE CAN WIN! / THE FEDERAL BOARD PROVIDES TRAINING / CONSULT THE LOCAL / RED CROSS HOME SERVICE SECTION. Dan Smith, artist. Baltimore: Thomsen-Ellis, Co. Color. 71 x 48. PL.

154. HELP CRUSH THE / MENACE OF THE SEAS / BUY LIBERTY BONDS / BUY QUICKLY BUY FREELY / RAINBOW DIVISION / SPECIAL / LIBERTY LOAN COMMITTEE. J. L. Grosse, artist. New York: Cloak, Suit and Skirt Industry Committee. Color. 71 x 46. Ak.

155. HELP / DELIVER / THE / GOODS / DO IT NOW. Herbert Paus, artist. New York: American Lithographic Co. Color. 103 x 71. Ak.

156. HELP HIM WIN BY / SAVING AND SERVING / BUY / WAR SAVINGS STAMPS. New York: American Lithographic Co., 1918. Color. 77 x 51.(Fig. 3.)

157. Same as 156. Ak.

158. HELP / THEM / KEEP YOUR / WAR SAVINGS / PLEDGE. Casper Emerson, Jr., artist. Washington: U. S. Treasury Dept. Color. 76 x 51. Mc.

159. Same as 158. Ak.

WW I: UNITED STATES

160. HELP / YOUR AMERICAN / RED CROSS / JOIN TODAY / NO FIELD SERVICE / REQUIRED OF MEMBERS / MEMBERSHIP DUES $1.00 UP. A. R. B., artist. New York: Schilling Press, Inc. Color. 115 x 76. Ak.

161. HOLD UP YOUR END! / WAR FUND WEEK / ONE HUNDRED MILLION DOLLARS. W. B. King, artist. Color. 70 x 57. Ak.

162. HONOR ROLL / THE FOLLOWING MEMBERS OF THIS ORGANIZATION HAVE ENROLLED AS MEMBERS OF THE RED CROSS FOR 1919 / . . . Color. 61 x 46. Ak.

163. HONOR ROLL / THE FOLLOWING PATRIOTIC MEN AND WOMEN / IN THIS ORGANIZATION HAVE BOUGHT BONDS OF THE / 4TH LIBERTY LOAN / . . . Chicago: Edwards & Deutsch Lith. Co. Color. 69 x 51. Ak.

164. HUN OR HOME? / BUY MORE / LIBERTY / BONDS. Henry Patrick Raleigh, artist. Chicago: Edwards & Deutsch Litho Co. Color. 76 x 51. Ak.

165. I AM TELLING YOU / ON JUNE 28TH I EXPECT YOU / TO ENLIST IN THE ARMY OF / WAR SAVERS TO BACK UP MY / ARMY OF FIGHTERS / W.S.S. ENLISTMENT. James Montgomery Flagg, artist. New York: American Lithographic Co. Color. 76 x 51. Ak.

166. "I SUMMON YOU / TO COMRADESHIP / IN THE RED CROSS" / WOODROW WILSON. Harrison C. Fisher, artist. New York: American Red Cross, 1918. Color. 101 x 76. Ak.

167. Same as 166. 70 x 51. Ak.

168. INVITATIONS TO HOMES / AND ENTERTAINMENTS / THE SPIRIT OF / WAR CAMP / COMMUNITY SERVICE / UNITED WAR WORK CAMPAIGN. New York: Heywood Strasser & Voight Litho. Co. Color. 76 x 51. (Fig. 10.)

169. JOAN OF ARC SAVED FRANCE / WOMEN OF AMERICA / SAVE YOUR COUNTRY / BUY WAR SAVINGS STAMPS. Haskell Coffin, artist. Washington: U. S. Treasury Dept. Color. 76 x 51. (Fig. 36.)

170. Same as 169. Ak.

171. JOIN / —ALL YOU NEED / IS A HEART / AND A DOLLAR. Color. 50 x 36. Ak.

172. JOIN THE / AIR SERVICE / AND / SERVE / IN FRANCE / DO IT / NOW. J. Paul Verrees, artist. Philadelphia: Ketterlinus, 1917. Color. 93 x 64. Ak.

173. KEEP 'EM / SMILING! / HELP / WAR CAMP / COMMUNITY SERVICE / "MORALE IS WINNING THE WAR" / UNITED WAR WORK CAMPAIGN. M. Leone Bracker, artist. 1918. Color. 101 x 71. Ak.

174. KEEP HIM FREE / BUY / WAR SAVINGS STAMPS. Charles Livingston Bull, artist. Philadelphia: United States Treasury Department. Color. 76 x 51. Ak.

175. KEEP IT COMING / "WE MUST NOT ONLY / FEED OUR SOLDIERS / AT THE FRONT BUT / THE MILLIONS OF / WOMEN & CHILDREN / BEHIND OUR LINES" / GEN. JOHN J. PERSHING / WASTE NOTHING. G. Illian, artist. New York: United States Food Administration. Color. 74 x 54. PL.

176. KNOWLEDGE WINS / PUBLIC LIBRARY / BOOKS / ARE / FREE. Dan Smith, artist. Baltimore: American Library Association. Color. 71 x 49. PL.

177. LEND! New York: Carey Print Litho. Color. 49 x 71. Ak.

178. LET'S END IT—QUICK / WITH LIBERTY BONDS. Maurice Ingres, artist. Cleveland: The Central Litho. Co. Color. 102 x 71. Mc. (Fig. 42.)

179. MONSTER / THRIFT FESTIVAL / . . . / POLO GROUNDS / . . . / SUNDAY, JUNE 2 / ENTIRE PROCEEDS FOR EDUCATIONAL FUND / NATIONAL WAR SAVINGS COMMITTEE FOR GREATER NEW YORK. New York: Carey Print Lith. Color. 92 x 180. Ak.

180. MUST / CHILDREN DIE / AND MOTHERS / PLEAD IN VAIN / ? / BUY MORE / LIBERTY BONDS. Walter H. Everett, artist. Color. 102 x 75.

181. MY DADDY BOUGHT ME A GOVERNMENT BOND / OF THE / THIRD LIBERTY LOAN / DID YOURS? New York: U.S. Printing & Lithograph Co. Color. 77 x 51. PL.

182. Same as 181. Ak.

183. MY SOLDIER / NOW I LAY ME DOWN TO SLEEP / I PRAY THE LORD MY SOUL TO KEEP. / GOD BLESS MY BROTHER GONE TO WAR / ACROSS THE SEAS, IN FRANCE, SO FAR. / OH, MAY HIS FIGHT FOR LIBERTY, / SAVE MILLIONS MORE THAN LITTLE ME / FROM CRUEL FATES OR RUTHLESS BLAST,— / AND BRING HIM SAFELY HOME AT LAST. / BUY UNITED STATES GOVERNMENT BONDS / THIRD LIBERTY LOAN. H. R. Green, artist. Buffalo: The Matthews-Northrup Works. Color. 106 x 72. Mc.

184. Same as 183. R.

185. Same as 183. Ak.

186. . . . 1918 / SPRING DRIVE / LIBERTY LOAN. Wilson Craig, artist. New York: Greenwich Litho. Co., 1918. Color. 71 x 51. Ak.

187. OH BOY! / THAT'S / THE GIRL! / THE / SALVATION ARMY / LASSIE / KEEP HER / ON THE / JOB / NOV. 11TH-18TH / 1918 / UNITED WAR WORK CAMPAIGN. G.M. Richards, artist. New York: Sackett & Wilhelms Corp., 1918. Color. 97 x 76. Ak.

188. ONLY THE NAVY CAN STOP THIS / W. A. Rogers, artist. New York: U. S. Navy Publicity Bureau. Color. 64 x 51. Ak.

189. OUR DADDY IS FIGHTING / AT THE FRONT FOR YOU / BACK HIM UP—BUY A / UNITED STATES GOV'T BOND OF THE / 2ND LIBERTY LOAN / OF 1917. Dewey, artist. New York: T. F. Moore Co., 1917. Color. 76 x 51. Mc. (Fig. 45.)

190. OVER THE TOP / FOR YOU / BUY U. S. GOV'T BONDS / THIRD LIBERTY LOAN. Sidney H. Riesenberg, artist. Philadelphia: Ketterlinus. Color. 76 x 51. Mc. (Frontispiece.)

191. Same as 190. PL.

192. Same as 190. Ak.

193. . . . / PVT. TREPTOW'S PLEDGE / HE HAD ALMOST REACHED / HIS GOAL WHEN A MACHINE / GUN

DROPPED HIM. / IN A POCKET OF HIS BLOUSE / THEY FOUND HIS PLEDGE / "I WILL FIGHT CHEERFULLY / AND DO MY UTMOST AS IF / THE WHOLE ISSUE OF THE / STRUGGLE DEPENDED ON ME / ALONE." / YOU WHO ARE / NOT CALLED UPON TO DIE— / SUBSCRIBE TO THE / FOURTH LIBERTY LOAN. C. LeRoy Baldridge, artist. Brooklyn: Robert Gair Company, 1918. Color. 76 x 51. Ak.

194. PROVIDE THE SINEWS OF WAR / BUY LIBERTY BONDS. Joseph Pennell, artist. New York: Heywood Strasser & Voight Litho. Co., 1918. B & W. 50 x 53. Ak.

195. RED CROSS / CHRISTMAS / ROLL CALL / DEC. 16-23RD / THE / GREATEST MOTHER / IN THE WORLD. Alonzo Earl Foringer, artist. Color. 102 x 71. Mc. (Fig. 26.)

196. Same as 195. Ak.

197. REMEMBER / ARGONNE / ... / AND / INVEST / VICTORY / LIBERTY LOAN / WOMAN'S / LIBERTY LOAN / COMMITTEE. J. M. H., artist. New York: Sackett & Wilhelms Corp. B & W. 77 x 51. PL.

198. REMEMBER / BELGIUM / BUY BONDS / FOURTH / LIBERTY / LOAN. Ellsworth Young, artist. New York: The United States Printing & Lithography Co. Color. 76 x 51. Mc. (Fig. 31.)

199. Same as 198. Ak.

200. REMEMBER! / THE FLAG OF LIBERTY / SUPPORT IT! / BUY / U. S. GOVERNMENT BONDS / 3RD LIBERTY LOAN. Griswold Tyng, artist. New York: Heywood Strasser & Voight Litho. Co. Color. 77 x 51. R.

201. Same as 200. PL.

202. Same as 200. Ak.

203. RING IT / AGAIN / BUY / U. S. GOV'T / BONDS / THIRD LIBERTY LOAN. New York: Sackett & Wilhelms Corp. Color. 77 x 51. PL.

204. Same as 203. Ak.

205. SAVE YOUR CHILD / FROM AUTOCRACY / AND POVERTY / BUY / WAR SAVINGS / STAMPS / ... Herbert Paus, artist. Washington: U.S. Treasury Department. Color. 76 x 51. Ak.

206. STRAIGHT FROM THE TRENCHES. ORIGINATED AND PRODUCED FOR THE LIBERTY LOAN COMMITTEE ENTIRELY BY MEMBERS OF THE AMERICAN EXPEDITIONARY FORCE / THE A.E.F. TO THE / PRESIDENT: / "IF THE FOLKS BACK / HOME FALL SHORT ON / THE BILLIONS YOU / NEED, MR. PRESIDENT, / CALL ON US FOR THE / BALANCE. WE LIKE OUR / PAY—BUT IF WE HAVE / TO WE CAN GO / WITHOUT IT. / YOURS FOR VICTORY, / A.E.F. / FRANCE, SEPT. 7, 1918 / 4TH LIBERTY LOAN. C. LeRoy Baldridge, artist. New York: Robert Gair Co., 1918. Color. 76 x 51.

207. SURE! / WE'LL / FINISH / THE JOB / VICTORY LIBERTY LOAN. Gerrit A. Beneker, artist. Chicago: Edwards & Deutsch Litho. Co., 1918. Color. 97 x 67. PL.

208. TEAM / WORK / WINS! / YOUR WORK / HERE MAKES / THEIR WORK / OVER THERE / POSSIBLE / WITH YOUR HELP THEY ARE INVINCIBLE / WITHOUT IT THEY ARE HELPLESS / WHATEVER YOU MAKE, MACHINE GUN OR HARNESS, CARTRIDGES OR HELMET, THEY ARE WAITING FOR IT. Roy Hull Still, artist. Washington: U. S. Army, Ordnance Department. Color. 102 x 71. Mc. (Fig. 14.)

209. THAT LIBERTY SHALL NOT / PERISH FROM THE EARTH / BUY LIBERTY BONDS / FOURTH LIBERTY LOAN. Joseph Pennell, artist. New York: Heywood Strasser & Voight Litho. Co. Color. 102 x 72. (Fig. 16.)

210. THE HUN—HIS MARK / **BLOT** IT **OUT** / WITH / LIBERTY BONDS. J. Allen St. John, artist. New York: Brett Litho. Co. Color. 108 x 72. Ak.

211. Same as 210. 76 x 51. Ak.

212. THE NAVY IS CALLING / ENLIST NOW. L. N. Britton, artist. Washington: U. S. Navy. Color. 105 x 73. Ak.

213. THE NAVY / NEEDS YOU! / DON'T READ / AMERICAN HISTORY— / MAKE IT! / U. S. NAVY RECRUITING STA-

WW I: UNITED STATES

TION. James Montgomery Flagg, artist. New York: H. C. Miner Litho. Co. Color. 102 x 71. Ak.

214. THE SPIRIT / OF / AMERICA / JOIN. Howard Chandler Christy, artist. Boston: American Red Cross, 1919. Color. 77 x 51. Ak.

215. THE TIDAL WAVE / JULY 4, 1918 / 95 SHIPS LAUNCHED. Cozz, artist. Philadelphia: Emergency Fleet Corp., 1918. Color. 77 x 52.

216. THINK—HAVE YOU BOUGHT YOUR LIMIT? / FOURTH LIBERTY LOAN. Color. 18 x 145. Ak.

217. THIRD RED CROSS ROLL CALL. Haskell Coffin, artist. New York: American Red Cross. Color. 76 x 51. Ak.

218. TO MAKE THE WORLD / A DECENT PLACE TO LIVE IN / DO YOUR PART—BUY U. S. GOVERNMENT BONDS / THIRD LIBERTY LOAN. Herbert Paus, artist. Buffalo: Niagara Litho. Co. Color. 91 x 142. PL.

219. Same as 218. Ak.

220. TRAVEL? / ADVENTURE? / ANSWER—JOIN THE MARINES! / ENLIST TODAY FOR 2-3 OR 4 YEARS. James Montgomery Flagg, artist. Color. 92 x 68.

221. 2 / INSPIRING / CABLEGRAMS / CHAIRMAN EDWARD N. HURLEY CABLES . . . / . . . / GENERAL PERSHING REPLIES. . . . C. Krieghoft, artist. Philadelphia: U. S. Shipping Board Emergency Fleet Corporation, 1918. Color. 110 x 80.

222. U-S-A BONDS / THIRD / LIBERTY LOAN / CAMPAIGN / BOY SCOUTS / OF AMERICA / WEAPONS FOR LIBERTY. Joseph Christian Leyendecker, artist. New York: American Lithographic Co. Color. 76 x 51. Mc.

223. Same as 222. Ak.

224. U. S. NAVY / OVER THERE. Albert Sterner, artist. New York: American Lithographic Co., 1917. Color. 180 x 101. Ak.

225. UNITED WAR WORK CAMPAIGN / THE BOYS' ONLY HOME / AWAY FROM HOME / 75% / 80%-85%-90%-95%-100% / OF OUR EMPLOYEES HAVE SUBSCRIBED. Color. 72 x 54.

226. UNIVERSAL MEMBERSHIP WEEK / RED CROSS CHRISTMAS ROLL CALL, DEC. 16-23RD. Color. 22 x 102. Ak.

227. WE BELONG / 100% / STRONG. 1919. Color. 61 x 45. Ak.

228. WHAT ARE YOU / DOING TO HELP? / JOIN YOUR / AMERICAN RED CROSS / SUBSCRIBING MEMBERSHIPS $2.00 UP. Gordon Grant, artist. Color. 97 x 64. Mc. (Fig. 40.)

229. Same as 228. Ak.

230. WHAT CAN YOU DO? / JOIN OUR RED CROSS / MEMBERSHIP INCLUDING RED CROSS MAGAZINE $2.00 / NO FIELD SERVICE REQUIRED. Color. 108 x 71. Ak.

231. WOMEN! / HELP AMERICA'S SONS / WIN THE WAR / BUY / U. S. GOVERNMENT BONDS / 2ND LIBERTY LOAN / OF 1917. R.H. Porteous, artist. Chicago: Edwards & Deutsch Litho. Co., 1917. Color. 76 x 51. Mc. (Fig. 44.)

232. YOU CAN HELP / AMERICAN RED CROSS. W. T. Benda, artist. New York: Alco-Gravure, Inc. Color. 77 x 51.

233. YOUR WAR / SAVINGS / PLEDGE / OUR BOYS MAKE GOOD / THEIR PLEDGE / ARE YOU KEEPING / YOURS? / W.S.S. / WAR SAVINGS STAMPS / ISSUED BY THE / UNITED STATES / GOVERNMENT. Color. 76 x 48.

234. Same as 233. Ak.

WORLD WAR II

CANADA

235. A MESSAGE FROM THE / PRIME MINISTER. 1941. Color. 67 x 48. Ak.

236. ALL CANADA / IS UNITED IN THIS / SINGLE PURPOSE / . . . / HELP FINISH THE JOB! / BUY VICTORY BONDS. Ottawa: National Committee, 1941. B & W. 57 x 42. Ak.

237. BEWARE / SPREADING VITAL INFORMATION / WILL UNDERMINE OUR WAR EFFORT / DO YOUR PART IN / SILENCE. Ottawa: Director of Public Information. Color. 62 x 47. Ak.

238. BEWARE / THE WALLS / HAVE EARS. Jac Leonard, artist. Ottawa: Wartime Information Board. Color. 62 x 46. Ak.

239. BUY VICTORY BONDS / INVEST AND / PROTECT / HELP / FINISH THE JOB. Franklin Arbuckle, artist. Color. 91 x 61. Ak.

240. Same as 239. 66 x 48. Ak.

241. CANADA— / HOLDS HIGH THE TORCH! / ... / HELP FINISH THE JOB! / BUY VICTORY BONDS. Ottawa: National Committee, 1941. B & W. 61 x 46. Ak.

242. CAN'T YOU SEE? / YOU MUST BUY / VICTORY BONDS. Al McLarell, artist. Color. 91 x 61. Ak.

243. CAN'T YOU SEE? / YOU MUST BUY / VICTORY BONDS. G. M. Rae, artist. Color. 91 x 61. Ak.

244. DOMINION OF CANADA / VICTORY BONDS / ARE BETTER THAN CASH / ... / HELP FINISH THE JOB! / BUY VICTORY BONDS. Ottawa: National Committee, 1941. B & W. 61 x 46. Ak.

245. GET YOUR TEETH / INTO THE / JOB. Nichol, artist. Ottawa: Wartime Information Board. Color. 69 x 46. R. (Fig. 59.)

246. GIVE US THE TOOLS AND WE WILL FINISH THE JOB / HELP FINISH THE JOB / BUY / VICTORY / BONDS. A. J. Casson, artist. Color. 66 x 48. Ak.

247. HELP / FINISH / THE / JOB! / BUY / VICTORY / BONDS. Color. 66 x 48. Ak.

248. IF THIS / WERE YOUR BOY / WOULDN'T YOU BACK HIM UP / TO THE LIMIT WITH / PLANES, BOMBS, GUNS? / ... Ottawa: National Committee, 1941. B & W. 61 x 46. Ak.

249. IT'S DO ... OR DIE ... CANADIANS! / ... / HELP FINISH THE JOB BUY VICTORY BONDS. Ottawa: National Committee, 1941. B & W. 57 x 42. Ak.

250. IT'S IN YOUR HANDS / HELP / FINISH / THE JOB / BUY VICTORY BONDS. L. Trevor, artist. Color. 67 x 48. Ak.

251. LEND / FOR THE KNOCKOUT BLOW! / ... / HELP FINISH THE JOB / BUY VICTORY BONDS! Ottawa: National Committee, 1941. B & W. 57 x 42. Ak.

252. LEND / TO FILL THE ENEMY'S SKY WITH BOMBERS / ... / HELP FINISH THE JOB / BUY VICTORY BONDS! Ottawa: National Committee, 1941. B & W. 58 x 42. Ak.

253. MEN OF VALOR / THEY FIGHT FOR YOU / MERCHANT NAVY—FOURTH ARM OF THE SERVICE. / OUTFIGHTING SUBMARINES AND DIVE BOMBERS IN A THREE DAY / BATTLE, CAPT. FRED S. SLOCOMBE, M.B.E., AND HIS HEROIC CREW / SUCCEEDED IN DELIVERING THE ICEBREAKER MONTCALM TO / MURMANSK AS A GIFT FROM CANADA TO THE U.S.S.R. Hubert Rogers, artist. Ottawa: War Information Board. Color. 92 x 61. R.

254. RUMOR / KILL IT! Ottawa: Director of Public Information. Color. 34 x 23. Ak.

255. SHOPTALK MAY BE / SABOTALK / THE WALLS HAVE EARS. G. R. Morris, artist. Ottawa: Wartime Information Board. Color. 62 x 46. Ak.

256. THIS IS WHY I AM / BUYING VICTORY / BONDS / ... Ottawa: National Committee, 1941. B & W. 57 x 42. Ak.

257. TO YOU THE TORCH IS THROWN / HELP / FINISH / THE JOB / BUY / VICTORY BONDS. Sampson, artist. Color. 92 x 61. Ak.

258. UNE INDISCRETION PEUT / CAUSER UNE CATASTROPHE / ... [One indiscretion can cause a catastrophe ...]. L. B. Jameson, artist. Ottawa: Affiche du Service de l'Information. Color. 76 x 51. R.

259. VICTORY / IS ON THE WAY! / ... / HELP FINISH THE JOB! / BUY VICTORY BONDS. Ottawa: National Committee, 1941. B & W. 62 x 46. Ak.

260. WARNING / THE SHARP EARS OF ENEMY AGENTS / ARE ALWAYS LISTENING / FOR SCRAPS OF INFORMA-

TION / DON'T LET YOUR CARELESS / TALK HELP THE ENEMY / . . . / BE ON YOUR GUARD. Ottawa: Director of Public Information. Color. 77 x 51. R.

261. WE DID IT BEFORE . . . / WE WILL DO IT AGAIN / . . . / HELP FINISH THE JOB! / BUY VICTORY / BONDS. Ottawa: National Committee, 1941. B & W. 61 x 46. Ak.

FRANCE

262. CETTE FOIS JUSQU'A / BERLIN [This time as far as Berlin.]. Color. 76 x 102. M. (Fig. 65.)

263. ENTRE LE MARTEAU . . . / . . . ET L'EN-CLUME! . . [Between the hammer and the anvil!] Jean Carlu, artist. Philadelphia: Republique Francaise—Commissariat a l'Information. Color. 54 x 37. R. (Fig. 35.)

264. PARIS! / 25 AOUT 1944 [Paris!—25 August 1944]. Le Service d'Information Allie. B & W. 51 x 76. M. (Fig. 64.)

GERMANY

265. ACHTUNG! / SOLDATEN! / DER HAUPTFEIND IM WESTEN IST DER JABO / . . . [Attention! Soldiers! The main enemy in the West is the attack bomber . . .]. Color. 42 x 30. P.

266. ADOLF HITLER IST DER SIEG! [Adolf Hitler is the victory!] R. Siehard Dill, artist. Reichenbach: Reichspropaganda-Leitung H. A. Pro., 1943. Color. 60 x 42. P.

267. BLEIBWEG! / AUSWASCHEN MACHT DIE WUNDE SCHLIMMER. / ICH LASS MICH VERBINDEN [Stay away! Washing aggravates the wound. I will have my wound bandaged]. Berlin: Berufsgenossenschaften e.V. durch die Unfallverhutungsbild. Color. 59 x 42. P.

268. DEIN WILLE: / LEISTUNG UND AUFSTIEG / DEIN HELFER: / DAS DEUTSCHE / LEISTUNGSER-TUCHTIGUNGSWERK / DER D A F / ANMELDUNG UND BERATUNG DURCH DEN BERUFSWALTER IM BETRIEB

/ ODER DIE KREISWALTUNGEN DER DEUTSCHEN ARBEITSFRONT [Your goal: achievement and advancement--Your helper: the German Job Training Program of the German Workers' Front--Registration and counseling through the job counselor in your firm or the District Office of the German Workers' Front]. W. Freres, artist. Berlin: Deutschen Arbeitsfront GmbH. Color. 60 x 42. P.

269. DER FUHRER RUFT / ZUM LEISTUNGSKAMPF / DER BETRIEBE 1939-40 / ... / DIE DEUTSCHE ARBEITSFRONT [The Fuhrer calls to the production competition 1939-40 ... The German Workers' Front]. Henzler, artist. Berlin: Deutschen Arbeitsfront. Color. 59 x 42. P.

270. DER REICHSMARSCHALL MIT SEINEN / LUFTWAFFEN-BEFEHLSHABERN / [section of poster missing] MANDIERENDEN / GENERALEN DER KORPS [The Reich Marshall with his Air Force commanders (and his?) Corps Commanders]. Berlin: August Scherl Nacht. B & W. 60 x 102. P.

271. DEUTSCHE MANNER IN DEN BETRIEBEN / MEINE ARBEITSKAMERADEN! / ... / HEIL HITLER / DR. ROBERT LEY ["German men in factories, firms, offices, my work comrades!" ... Heil Hitler—Dr. Robert Ley]. Berlin: Deutschen Arbeitsfront. Color. 59 x 42. P.

272. DIE DEUTSCHE ARBEITSFRONT / DEUTSCHE WINZER / WERBEN FUR DEUTSCHEN WEIN [The German Workers' Front—German winegrowers advertise German wine]. Berlin: Derlag der Deutschen Arbeitsfront. Color. 85 x 60. P.

273. FAHNEN / FLAGGEN UND / STANDARTEN / DER / DEUTSCHEN WEHRMACHT ... [Flags, pennants, and standards of the German army ...]. Die Wehrmacht. Color. 34 x 25. P.

274. FUR WISSEN UND UNTERHALTUNG: / DIENE / WERKBUCHEREI / DIE DEUTSCHE ARBEITSFRONT—AMT DEUTSCHES VOLKSBILDUNGSWERK [For knowledge and entertainment: see your library in your place of employment—The German Workers' Front Office for People's Education]. Berlin: Deutschen Arbeitsfront GmbH. Color. 60 x 42. P.

275. HARTE ZEITEN / HARTE PFLICHTEN / HARTE HERZEN [Hard times, hard duties, hard hearts]. Color. 86 x 61. P. (Fig. 63.)

276. [HITLER, THE LIBERATOR (Ukranian)]. Dresden: Kunstanstalten May. Color. 84 x 60. P. (Fig. 60.)

277. LADEN EINES TORPEDOS IM U-BOOT / AUF ENGSTEM RAUM MUSSEN IN U-BOOTEN DIE SCHWEREN, LANGEN TORPEDOS BEWEGT UND DABEI PFLEGLICH BEHANDELT / . . . [Loading of a torpedo in a submarine—In the narrow space of a submarine the heavy and long torpedoes must be moved and handled with great caution . . .]. E. Gotz, artist. Berlin: Des Oberkommandos der Kriegsmarine. Color. 51 x 71. P.

278. MIT KRAFT DURCH FREUDE / ZUM / WINTERSPORT / . . . / DIE DEUTSCHE ARBEITSFRONT GAU THURINGEN [With strength through joy to the wintersport areas . . . The German Workers' Front Thuringia]. E. W. Friedrich, artist. Weimar: The German Workers' Front Thuringia. Color. 92 x 63. P.

279. 'N HALBEN TAG VERLOREN! / TRUPPENTRANSPORTE UBER . . .' / FEIND / HORT / MIT! ['Lost half a day! Troop transports via . . .' —The enemy listens in!] Color. 60 x 42. P.

280. SANITATSDIENST AN BORD / DIE FURSORGE FUR KRANKE UND VERWUNDETE LIEGT AN BORD DEM SANITATSPERSONAL OB. AUF ALLEN SCHIFFEN BEFINDET SICH EIN ARZT / . . . [Medical aid men on board—The care for the sick and wounded on board is the duty of the medical personnel. All ships have a doctor on board . . .]. Karl Blossfeld, artist. Berlin: Des Oberkommandos der Kriegsmarine. Color. 51 x 71. P.

281. U-BOOT-BUNKER / GEWALTIGE BAUTEN SIND AN DER ATLANTIK-KUSTE ZUM SCHUTZE UNSERER U-BOOT-STUTZPUNKLE GEGEN LUFT / . . . [Submarine bunker—impressive fortifications have been built along the Atlantic coast for the protection of our submarine bases against air attacks . . .]. E. Gotz, artist. Berlin: Des Oberkommandos der Kriegsmarine. Color. 51 x 71. P.

282. UNERSCHROCKENE FRONTSOLDATEN, NACH DEM WILLEN DES FUHRERS / MIT DEN MODERNSTEN WAFTEN AUSGERUSTET, ERKAMPFEN SICH DES BE- / FOHLENE ANGRIFFSZIEL. / IHR HELDENTUM WIRD IN DER GESCHICHTE EWIG FORTBESTEHEN [Intrepid front soldiers, equipped with the most modern weapons, as ordered by the Fuhrer, fight their way toward the designated objective. Their heroism will endure forever in history]. P. K. Jager, artist. Color. 91 x 65. P.

283. UNIFORMEN / DES DEUTSCHEN HEERES / DIENSTGRADABZEICHEN USW. / TAFEL 1 / ... [Uniforms of the German Army—Rank insignia, etc.—Plate 1 ...]. Color. 34 x 25. P.

284. UNIFORMEN / DES DEUTSCHEN HEERES / DIENSTGRADABZEICHEN USW. / TAFEL 2 / ... [Uniforms of the German Army—Rank insignia, etc.—Plate 2 ...]. Color. 34 x 25. P.

285. UNIFORMEN / DER DEUTSCHEN / LUFTWAFFE / DIENSTGRADABZEICHEN USW. / TAFEL I / ... [Uniforms of the German Air Force—Rank insignia, etc.—Plate I ...]. Color. 34 x 25. P.

286. UNIFORMEN / DER DEUTSCHEN / LUFTWAFFE / DIENSTGRADABZEICHEN USW. / TAFEL II / ... [Uniforms of the German Air Force—Rank insignia, etc.—Plate II ...]. Color. 34 x 25. P.

287. UNTEROFFIZIER / IM HEER / DEIN BERUF! / MELDUNG FUR 4½ ODER 12 JAHRIGE DIENSTZEIT BEIM WEHRBEZIRKSKOMMANDO [Noncommissioned officer in the Army—your job! Enlistment for 4½ or 12 years at the Army District Command—Infantryman]. Land Wehr Mann, artist. Leipzig: Meissner & Buch. Color. 59 x 42. P. (Fig. 62.)

288. VORPOSTENBOOT AUF WEITER SEE / WEIT DRAUFSEN STEUERT DAS DEUTSCHE VORPOSTEN-BOOT SEINEN KURS UND SICHERT DAS KUSTEN-VORFELD. GLEICH / ... [Picket boat on high seas—Far out, the German picket boat steers its course and secures the coastal waters ...]. Ernst Rusch, artist. Berlin: Des Oberkommandos der Kriegsmarine, 1943. Color. 51 x 71. P.

Wochenspruchen der Nationalsozialistische Deutsche Arbeiterparte (NSDAP) [weekly slogans of the National German Workers' Party]. The following posters, numbers 289-415, in this weekly series are listed in chronological order. Two colors, black and red, were used in printing each poster, and they measure 35 x 25 cm. They were the gift of Forrest C. Pogue.

289. FUHRER— / IN DEINEN HANDEN / LEIGT DAS SCHICKSAL VON / MILLIONEN, DIE IN DEINEM / HERZEN WOHNEN, DENEN / DU EIN GLAUBE BIST. / FUHRE UNS! [Fuhrer—in your hands lies the fate of millions who live in your heart and who believe in you. Lead us!] 1938. P. (Fig. 18.)

290. DAS / DEUTSCHE / VOLK / BRAUCHT NUR FEINE INNERE EI-/NKIGKEIT ZU WAHREN U, IN BEDIN- / GUNGSLOSER TREUE ZUM FUHRER / ZU BEHARREN, UND ES WIRD ALLES / VERWIRKLICHT WERDEN, WAS DIE GROSSEN DEUTSCHEN AUS WEIT MEHR / ALS EINEM JAHRTAUSEND ALS / GROSSE UNSERES VOLKES U KUHM / UNSERES KEICHES ERSEHNTEN. GAULEITER STAATSRAT GROHE ["The German people need only to preserve their inner unity and to persevere in unconditional loyalty to the Fuhrer and everything will be realized that the great Germans of more than one thousand years ago had longed for as the greatness of our peoples and the glory of our Empire." District Chief Staatsrat Grohe]. Feb. 28-March 6, 1938 (10th week). P.

291. DIE LETZTE / ULNSTERBLICHKEIT / IN DIESER WELT / LIEGT IN DER / EWIGKEIT / DES VOLKSTUMS. / ADOLF HITLER ["The final immortality in this world lies in the eternity of the national culture." Adolf Hitler]. Willi Kleine, artist. March 14-20, 1938 (12th week). P.

292. NUR / DIE GROSSE DES / OPFERS WIRD EIN-/MAL DIE GROSSE / DES SIEGES / OFFENBAREN. / WAS LEICHT / ERKAMPFT, WIRD / LEICHT VERGESSEN. / ADOLF HITLER ["Only the greatness of the sacrifice will some day reveal the greatness of the victory. Whatever is easily conquered, is easily forgotten." Adolf Hitler]. March 21-27, 1938 (13th week). P.

293. ZUM VOLKSENTSCHEID / 10-4-1938 / DEUTSCHES VOLK IN OSTERREICH, / PREUSSEN, BAYERN, IN ALLEN / DEUTSCHEN GAUEN EINIG, UND / FREI DURCH ADOLF HITLER! / DEM FUHRER UNSER / JA [On the occasion of the people's decision, 10 April 1938, German people in Austria, Prussia, Bavaria, in all German districts, united and free through Adolf Hitler! To the Fuhrer our yes]. Willi Kleine, artist. April 4-10, 1938 (15th week). P.

294. JEDER DEUTSCHE / JUNGE, JEDES / DEUTSCHE MADCHEN: SIE / MUSSEN DURCHDRUNGEN SEIN / VON DEM HEI-/LIGEN PFLICHT-/BEWUSSTSEIN / REPRASENTANTEN / UNSERES VOLKES / ZU WERDEN. / ADOLF HITLER ["Every German boy and every German girl: They must be filled with a holy sense of duty to represent our nation." Adolf Hitler]. May 9-15, 1938 (20th week). P.

295. DIE STARKE DER / STRAATEN BERUHT / AUF DEN GROSSEN / MANNERN, DIE / IHNEN ZUR RECH-/TEN STUNDE GE-/BOREN WERDEN. / FRIEDRICH DER GROSSE ["The strength of the states rests on the great men who are born to them at the right hour." Frederick the Great]. May 16-22, 1938 (21st week). P.

296. WEIL WIR / EINIG / SIND, SIND WIR / STARK, / WEIL WIR STARK / SIND, SIND WIR / FREI! / HERMANN GORING ["Because we are unified, we are strong. Because we are strong, we are free." Hermann Goring]. May 23-29, 1938 (22nd week). P.

297. WIR / MENSCHEN / HABEN NICHT DARUBER / ZU RECHTEN, WARUM DIE / VORSEHUNG DIE / RASSEN SCHUF, SONDERN / NUR ZU ERKENNEN, DASS / SIE DEN BESTRAFT, DER / IHRE SCHOPFUNG / MISSACHTET. / ADOLF HITLER ["We human beings are not to question why Providence created races; we are only to recognize that Providence punishes him who disregards their divine creation." Adolf Hitler]. May 30-June 5, 1938 (23rd week). P.

298. DAS IST DIE SCHON-/STE AUFGABE VON / KRAFT DURCH FREUDE: / DEM SCHAFFENDEN / DEUTSCHEN MEN-/SCHEN MUT UND / LEBENSWILLEN ZU / GEBEN—DR. ROBERT LEY ["This is the finest duty of

'Strength through Joy': to give the working German courage and a will to live." Dr. Robert Ley]. June 6-12, 1938 (24th week). P.

299. RASTLOS VORWARTS / MUSST DU STREBEN, / NIE ERMUDET STILLE STEHN, / WILLST DU DIE VOLLEN- / DUNG SEHN; MUSST INS / BREITE DICH ENTFALTEN, / SOLL SICH DIR DIE WELT / GESTALTEN; IN DIE TIEFE / MUSST DU STEIGEN, SOLL / SICH DIR DAS WESEN ZEIGEN / FRIEDRICH VON SCHILLER ["You must strive relentlessly forward, never stand still, exhausted, if you wish to see your task completed; you must grow steadily in order to shape the world; you must descend into the depths if the essence of reality is to show itself in you." Friedrich von Schiller]. June 14-19, 1938 (25th week). P.

300. SONNENWENDE / DRUM MUTIG DREIN / UND NIMMER BLEICH / DENN GOTT / IST ALLENTHALBEN: DIE FREIHEIT UND DAS / HIMMELREICH / GEWINNEN / KEINE HALBEN! / ERNST MORITZ ARNDT ["Solstice— forward with courage, never blanch, for God is everywhere: the freedom and the heavenly kingdom are not won by the halfhearted." Ernst Moritz Arndt]. June 20-26, 1938 (26th week). P.

301. DER / VOLKISCHE / STAAT / WIRD DAFUR SORGEN MUSSEN, / DURCH EINE PASSENDE ERZIE-/HUNG DER JUGEND DEREINST / DAS FUR DIE LETZTEN UND GROSS-/TEN ENTSCHEIDUNGEN AUF DIE-/SEM ERD- BALL REIFE GESCHLECHT / ZU ERHALTEN. / ADOLF HITLER ["The nation-state will have as its task, through a fitting education of youth, the formation of a generation able to face the last and greatest decisions on this planet." Adolf Hitler]. June 27-July 3, 1938 (27th week). P.

302. KUNST / IST HOCHSTER / AUSDRUCK DER SCHOP-/FERISCHEN KRAFTE EINES / VOLKES.—DER / KUNSTLER / IST IHR BEGNADETER / SINNGEBER. / DR. JOSEF GOEBBELS ["Art is the highest expression of the creative powers of a nation.—The artist is blessed with the task to give it meaning." Dr. Josef Goebbels]. July 4-10, 1938 (28th week). P.

303. WAS UNZAHLIGEN UNSERER / SOGENANNTEN GEBILDETEN / SCHICHTEN FRUHER ALS ETWAS / ZWEITWERTIGES / ERSCHIEN, IST / HEUTE AUFGEWERTET WORDEN— / DER SPATEN WURDE ZUM / SYMBOL EINER NEUEN / GEMEINSCHAFT. / ADOLF HITLER ["That which earlier had seemed secondary to innumerable members of our so-called educated classes has today been revalued and upgraded. The spade became the symbol of a new community." Adolf Hitler]. July 11-17, 1938 (29th week). P.

304. NUR WER SELBER AM EIGENEN / LEIBE FUHLT—WAS ES HEISST-/DEUTSCHER ZU SEIN OHNE DEM / LIEBEN VATERLANDE ANGEHO-/REN ZU DURFEN, VERMAG DIE / TIEFE SEHNSUCHT ZU ERMESSEN, / DIE ZU ALLEN ZEITEN IM HER-/ZEN DER VOM MUT-TERLANDE / GETRENNTEN KINDER BRENNT. / ADOLF HITLER ["Only he who himself feels what it means to be a German without being allowed to belong to the Fatherland is capable of judging the deep yearning that burns at all times in the hearts of those children separated from the Motherland." Adolf Hitler]. July 18-24, 1938 (30th week). P.

305. WIR WISSEN, DASS WIR / AUF EIGENE / KRAFT / GESTELLT SIND, DASS WIR / NICHTS HABEN ZUM AUFBAU / UNSERER ZUKUNFT ALS DIE / KRAFTE UNSERER HANDE, / UNSERES GEISTES, / UNSERES WILLENS / BERNHARD RUST ["We know that we depend on our own strength, that we have nothing to build our future with other than the strength of our hands, our minds, our wills." Bernhard Rust]. Willi Kleine, artist. July 25-31, 1938 (31st week). P.

306. DER / DEUTSCHE LEBENSRAUM / IST OHNE KOLONIALE ERGANZUNG ZU / KLEIN, UM EINE UNGESTORTE, SICHERE, / DAUERNDE ERNAHRUNG UNSERES / VOLKES ZU GARANTIEREN. ES IST / DAHER DIE FORDERUNG NACH EI-/NEM DEM REICH GEHORENDEN / KOLONIALBESITZ EINE IN UNSERER / WIRTSCHAFTLICHEN NOT BEGRUNDE-/TE U, DIE EINSTELLUNG DER ANDERN / MACHTE ZU DIESER FORDERUNG EI-/NE EINFACH NICHT

VERSTANDLICHE. / ADOLF HITLER ["The German living-space is, without colonial supplement, too small to guarantee an undisturbed, safe and lasting food supply for our people. Therefore the demand for a colonial possession as part of an empire is one founded on economic need, and the attitude of other powers toward this demand is simply incomprehensible." Adolf Hitler]. Aug. 8-14, 1938 (33rd week). P.

307. JEDE VERSUNDIGUNG / GEGEN DIE / RASSENREINHEIT / IST EINE / VERSUNDIGUNG GEGEN / GOTTES WILLEN / UND GEGEN DIE / SCHOPSUNGSORDNUNG / HANS SCHEMM ["Each offense against racial purity is a sin against God's will and against the divine order of creation." Hans Schemm]. Aug. 15-21, 1938 (34th week). P.

308. POLITIK / IST NICHTS ANDERES, / ALS DER VERSUCH, / DAS SCHICKSAL / EINES VOLKES / ZUM GUTEN / ZU MEISTERN. / DR. GOEBBELS ["Politics is nothing other than the attempt to direct the fate of the people toward a common good." Dr. Goebbels]. Aug. 22-28, 1938 (35th week). P.

309. WER EHRLOS IST, / IST FRIEDLOS—UND / NUR WO EIN STARKES / SCHWERT DEN FRIEDEN / SCHUTZT, KANN EIN / VOLK DIE GUTER SEINER / ARBEIT SELBST IN FRIEDEN / VERZEHREN. / HERMANN GORING ["The dishonorable man is without peace—and only where a strong sword protects peace can a nation enjoy the fruits of its labor in peace." Hermann Goring]. Aug. 29-Sept. 4, 1938 (36th week). P.

310. WIR BLICKEN VOLLER STOLZ / ZURUCK AUF DIE LEISTUNGEN / DIE DAS / DEUTSCHE / VOLK DURCH SEINE / ARBEIT IM ZEICHEN DES / NATIONALSOZIALISMUS / VOLLBRACHT HAT / RUDOLF HESS / STELLVERTRETER DES FUHRERS ["We look back proudly at the achievements that the German nation has gained through its work under the symbol of National Socialism." Rudolf Hess, Deputy of the Fuhrer]. Willi Kleine, artist. Sept. 5-11, 1938 (37th week). P.

311. NURNBERG / MOGEN DIE ZEITEN / UBER UNS SCHREITEN / EIN JUNGES VOLK / STEHT IMMER

BEREIT / WENN WIR VERGEHEN, / WIRD NEUES STEHEN / HEUTE UND BIS IN / DIE EWIGKEIT [Nuremberg—May the times pass over us—a young nation is always prepared. When we pass on, a new nation will stand—today and throughout eternity]. Sept. 12-18, 1938 (38th week). P.

312. DEUTSCH IS ALLES / WAS DURCH DEUTSCHE / GESCHICHTE GEGANGEN / IST—DEUTSCHES BLUT IN / SICH HAT UND DEUTSCHE / SPRACHE SPRICHT / KONRAD HENLEIN ["German are all who have gone through German history, in whom flow German blood, and who speak the German language." Konrad Henlein]. Sept. 19-25. 1938 (39th week). P.

313. GLEICHES / BLUT / GEHORT IN EIN / GEMEINSAMES / REICH! ADOLF HITLER ["Common blood belongs in a common empire!" Adolf Hitler]. Sept. 26-Oct. 2, 1938 (40th week). P.

314. ES GIBT / NICHTS / FURCHTERLICHERES FUR / EIN VOLK, ALS SEINE / EHRE PREISZUGEBEN. UNSERE EHRE / WERDEN WIR NIE, NIE / MEHR PREISGEBEN. / HERMANN GORING / REICHSPARTEITAG 1938 NURNBERG ["There is nothing more horrible for a nation than to surrender its honor. We will never, never again, surrender our honor." Hermann Goring, Party Rally, Nuremberg, 1938]. Willi Kleine, artist. Oct. 3-9, 1938 (41st week). P.

315. MEIN BISHERIGES / LEBEN IST EIN / KAMPF / GEWESEN—ABER / KAPITULIERT HABE / ICH NIEMALS UND / MEIN ZIEL / HABE ICH ERREICHT / ADOLF HITLER ["My life until now has been a struggle, but I never capitulated and I reached my goal." Adolf Hitler]. Oct. 10-16, 1938 (42nd week). P.

316. MAN / BETTELT NICHT / UM EIN RECHT! / FUR EIN RECHT / KAMPFT MAN / ADOLF HITLER ["One does not beg for a right! One fights for a right!" Adolf Hitler]. Oct. 17-23, 1938 (43rd week). P.

317. BLUT IST STARKER / ALS FEINDLICHE / MACHT, UND WAS / DEUTSCH / SEIN WILL, MUSS / DEUTSCHLAND / GEHOREN! [Blood is stronger than hostile enemy power, and

whatever wishes to be German must belong to Germany!] Oct. 24-30, 1938 (44th week). P.

318. DIE BUCHER ALS DIE WEG-/BEGLEITER DER VOLKER, HABEN / ZU ALLEN ZEITEN NICHT NUR / VERGANGENE GROSSE EPOCHEN / VERHERRLICHT, SONDERN AUCH / KOMMENDE GROSSE EPOCHEN / GEAHNT, ANGEKUNDIGT UND / VORBEREITER. / IM BUCH / OFFENBART / EIN VOLK / SICH SELBST. / DR. JOSEF GOEBBELS ["Books, as companions of nations, have always not only glorified great past eras, but have also sensed, announced, and prepared future great epochs. In books a nation reveals itself." Dr. Josef Goebbels]. Oct. 31-Nov. 6, 1938 (45th week). P.

319. 9. NOVEMBER 1923 / GEBOREN ALS DEUTSCHER, / GELEBT ALS KAMPFER, / GEFALLEN ALS HELD, / AUFERSTANDEN ALS VOLK! [9 November 1923—Born as a German, lived as a fighter, died in battle as a hero, resurrected as a nation!] Nov. 7-13, 1938 (46th week). P.

320. WER SEIN / VOLK / LIEBT, BEWEIST ES / EINZIG DURCH DIE / OPFER / DIE ER FUR DIESES / ZU BRINGEN / BEREIT / IST. / ADOLF HITLER ["He who loves his nation proves his love only through the sacrifices he is prepared to make for it." Adolf Hitler]. Nov. 14-20, 1938 (47th week). P.

321. EIN / VOLK / DAS SEIN / BLUT / VOM JUDEN / FREIHALT, / WIRD EWIG / LEBEN. / JULIUS STREICHER ["A nation whose blood is kept free from Jewish taint will live forever." Julius Streicher]. Nov. 21-27, 1938 (48th week). P.

322. 5 JAHRE / KRAFT DURCH FREUDE / KRAFT DURCH FREUDE— / IST NICHT LEDIGLICH EINE FREI- / ZEITORGANISATION—SONDERN / SIE IST EINE NATIONALSOZIA-/LISTICHE GEMEINSCHAFT / DIE AN DEM WERDEN EINER / NEUEN LEBENGESTALTUNG / MITWIRKT UND DIE NEUE GE-/SELLSCHAFTSORDNUNG HERSTELLT. / DR. ROBERT LEY [5 years—Strength through Joy—" 'Strength through Joy' is not simply a recreational organization—rather it is a national socialistic community that contributes to the realization of a new

way of life and that establishes a new social order." Dr. Robert Ley]. Nov. 28-Dec. 4, 1938 (49th week). P.

323. ES / HAT NUR DER / EIN RECHT, / IN DER / VOLKSGEMEINSCHAFT / ZU LEBEN / DER BEREIT IST, / FUR DIE / VOLKSGEMEINSCHAFT / ZU ARBEITEN. / ALFRED ROSENBERG ["Only he has a right to live as a member of the nation who is prepared to work for the nation." Alfred Rosenberg]. Dec. 5-11, 1938 (50th week). P.

324. SOLANGE VOLK / UND FUHRER / EINS SIND, WIRD / DEUTSCHLAND / UNUBERWINDBAR SEIN. / DER HERR SANDTE UNS DEN / FUHRER / NICHT DAMIT WIE UNTERGEHEN, / SONDERN DAMIT DEUTSCHLAND / AUFERSTEHE / HERMANN GORING ["As long as the nation and the Fuhrer are one, Germany will be invincible. The Lord sent us the Fuhrer not in order for us to perish, but in order for Germany to rise again"—Hermann Goring]. Dec. 12-18, 1938 (51st week). P.

325. WIR ALLE IN / DEUTSCHLAND / KONNEN UNS IN / DIESEM JAHR ZUM / ERSTEN MAL WIRK-/LICH FREUEN AUF DAS / WEIHNACHTSFEST / ES SOLL FUR UNS ALLE / EIN WAHRES / FEST DES FRIEDENS / SEIN. / ADOLF HITLER ["For the first time, all of us in Germany can truly look forward to Christmas—It should be a true holiday of peace for us all." Adolf Hitler]. Willi Kleine, artist. Dec. 19-25, 1938 (52nd week). P.

326. DIE MENSCHEN / KOMMEN, UND / MENSCHEN STERBEN. / ABER DIESE GEMEINSCHAFT, / AUS DER SICH IMMER WIEDER / DIE NATION / ERNEUERT, SIE SOLL EWIG SEIN / ADOLF HITLER ["Men come and men go—but this community in which the nation always renews itself, it shall be eternal." Adolf Hitler]. Willi Kleine, artist. Dec. 26-31, 1938 (53rd week). P.

327. DAS / NEUE / JAHR / SOLL UNS ERFULLT SE-/HEN VON EINEM / NEUEN, HEILIGEN / EIFER, ZU ARBEITEN / UND EINZUTRETEN / FUR UNSER VOLK. / ADOLF HITLER ["The new year should see us filled with a new, holy zeal to work and to defend our nation." Adolf Hitler]. Jan. 2-8, 1939 (1st week). P.

328. NIEMAND / KANN VON EINER / KOMMENDEN / GENERATION / ERWARTEN, / WAS DIE LEBENDE / VERSAUMT. / DR. GOEBBELS ["You cannot expect the coming generation to make up for the failures of the present one." Dr. Goebbels]. Jan. 9-15, 1939 (2nd week). P.

329. WER GLAUBEN / IM HERZEN HAT, / DER HAT DIE / STARKSTE KRAFT / DER WELT. / ADOLF HITLER ["He who has faith in his heart has the greatest strength in the world." Adolf Hitler]. Jan. 15-21, 1939. P.

330. GROSSE / MENSCHEN / SIND / TATGEWORDENE / WUNSCHE / IRHES / VOLKES. / HANS SCHEMM ["Great humans are the extension of the hopes of their nation." Hans Schemm]. Jan. 22-28, 1939. P.

331. NUR DIE NATION / DIE IHRE EHRE HOCHHALT, / VERMAG AUF DIE DAUER / ZU BESTEHEN. / DEUTSCHLAND WIRD / BESTEHEN—DANK / DEM FUHRER. RUDOLF HESS ["Only the nation that upholds its honor is capable of enduring as time passes. Germany will endure—Thanks to the Fuhrer." Rudolf Hess]. Jan. 29-Feb. 4, 1939. P.

332. DIE TREUE / IST EINE / ANGELEGENHEIT / DES HERZENS / NIEMALS / DES VERSTANDES. / HEINRICH HIMMLER ["Loyalty is a matter of the heart, never of the intellect." Heinrich Himmler]. Feb. 5-11, 1939. P.

333. DIE LEISTUNG / ALLEIN / UNTERSCHEIDE / DEN EINEN VOM / ANDEREN / ROBERT LEY ["Achievement alone should distinguish one man from another." Robert Ley.]. Feb. 12-18, 1939. P.

334. TIEFER SOLL KEINE GLOCKE / JE TONEN UBER UNS ALS / DAS WORT VOLK! / WALTER FLEX ["Let no bell toll more deeply above us all than the word Nation!" Walter Flex]. Feb. 19-25, 1939. P.

335. SOLANG EIN FEIND NOCH / IN GERMANIEN TROTZT, / IST HASS MEIN AMT UND / MEINE TUGEND RACHE! / HENRICH VON KLEIST ["As long as an enemy resists on Germany's soil, hate is my duty and my virtue vengeance!" Henrich von Kleist]. March 5-11, 1939. P.

336. HELDENGEDENKTAG 1939 / UBER GRABER VORWARTS! [Heroes' Commemoration Day 1939—Forward over the graves!]. March 12-18, 1939. P.

337. DER HERRGOTT HAT DIE VOLKER / GESCHAFFEN / WAS ABER DER HERRGOTT / EINIGT, SOLLEN DIE MENSCHEN / NIEMALS TRENNEN ADOLF HITLER ["God created the nations--but what God united, men shall never separate." Adolf Hitler]. March 19-25, 1939. P.

338. WER / DEN HIMMEL / WILL GEWINNEN, / MUSS EIN RECHTER / KAMPFER SEIN! / EMANUEL GEIBEL ["To win heaven, you must be a true fighter!" Emanuel Geibel]. March 26-April 1, 1939. P.

339. MAN MUSS / DAS UNMOGLICHE / VERLANGEN, DAMIT / DAS MOGLICHE / GELEISTET WIRD. / HELMUTH VON MOLTKE ["One must demand the impossible to get the possible accomplished." Helmuth von Moltke]. April 2-8, 1939. P.

340. WAS MICH NICHT / UMBRINGT, / MACHT MICH STARKER. / FRIEDRICH NIETZSCHE ["Whatever does not destroy me makes me stronger." Friedrich Nietzsche]. April 9-15, 1939. P.

341. EINE / FEIGE / POLITIK HAT / NOCH IMMER / UNGLUCK / GEBRACHT. / OTTO VON BISMARCK ["Cowardly statesmanship has always led to disaster." Otto von Bismarck]. April 23-29, 1939. P.

342. DER GROSSE MANN GEHT / SEINER ZEITVORAUS, / DER KLUGE GEHT MIT IHR / AUFALLEN WEGEN, / DER SCHLAUKOPF BEUTET / SIE GEHORIGAUS, / DER DUMMKOPF STELLT / SICH IHR ENTGEGEN. / ERNST MORITZ ARNDT ["The great man precedes his time; the wise man adjusts to it in all its ways: the smart man takes full advantage of it; the dullard opposes it." Ernst Moritz Arndt]. May 7-13, 1939. P.

343. ES GIBT / IM VOLKERLEBEN / JAHRE, IN DENEN / DIE ENTSCHEIDUNG / UBER / SEIN / ODER / NICHTSEIN / FUR KOMMENDE / JAHRHUNDERTEFALLT. / ADOLF HITLER—7.2.34 ["In the life of nations there are years which

bring decisions over life and death for the coming centuries." Adolf Hitler—7 Feb. 1934]. May 14-20, 1939. P.

344. DIE / ARBEIT / EHRT DIE FRAU / WIE DEN MANN. / DAS KIND ABER / ADELT DIE MUTTER. / ADOLF HITLER ["Work dignifies woman as well as man. The child, however, honors the mother." Adolf Hitler]. May 21-27, 1939. P.

345. WER IN DEN ZEITEN GROSSER VATER-/LANDISCHER KAMPFE GANZ UNBEFANGEN / UND LEIDENSCHAFT-SLOS ZU BLEIBENVER-/MAG, DER VERDIENT NICHT, SIE ZU ERLEBEN. / HEINRICH VON TREITSCHKE ["Men who can remain totally unmoved and dispassionate in times of great national struggles do not deserve to live in them." Heinrich von Treitschke]. Fuchs, artist. May 28-June 3, 1939. P.

346. GAUTAG 1939 / WESTMARK / BOLLWERK DER / HERZEN UND HIRNE [District Day 1939—Westmark, bulwark of hearts and minds]. June 4-10, 1939. P.

347. FLEISS UND / ARBEIT ALLEIN / SCHAFFEN NICHT / DAS LEBEN, WENN SIE / SICH NICHT VERMAHLEN / MIT DER KRAFT UND DEM / WILLEN / EINES— / VOLKES / ADOLF / HITLER ["Diligence and hard work alone do not master life if they do not unite themselves with the strength and purpose of a nation." Adolf Hitler]. June 11-17, 1939. P.

348. LASS / WAS STERBEN MUSS / SINKEN UND MODERN / WAS KRAFT HAT / WAS LICHT HAT / WILL STEIGEN UND / LODERN / GERHARD / SCHUMANN ["Let go down and decay what must die; whatever has strength, whatever has light will rise and blaze"—Gerhard Schumann]. June 18-24, 1939. P.

349. ALLE / SCHWANKUNGEN SIND / AM ENDE ZU ERTRAGEN, / ALLE SCHICKSALSSCHLAGE / ZU UBER-WINDEN, / WENN EIN / GESUNDES BAUERNTUM / VORHANDEN IST / ADOLF HITLER AM 5. APRIL 1933 ["In the end, all ups and downs can be endured, all blows of fate overcome, if there exists a healthy peasantry." Adolf Hitler on 5 April 1933]. June 25-July 1, 1939. P.

WW II: GERMANY

350. UNSER / WAR DER / GLAUBE / UNSER IST DER / WILLE / ADOLF HITLER ["Ours was the faith—ours is the will." Adolf Hitler]. July 9-15, 1939. P.

351. GANZ BIN ICH NUR / WAS ICH BIN / WENN ICH SCHAFFE. / RICHARD WAGNER ["Only when I create am I completely myself." Richard Wagner]. July 16-22, 1939 (on the occasion of the opening of the Bayreuth Festival, 1939). P.

352. DEN GESETZEN / DES LEBENS GE-/HORCHEN HEISST / EIN GROSSES / SCHICKSAL / BEGREIFEN. / ALFRED ROSENBERG ["To obey the laws of life is to understand a great destiny." Alfred Rosenberg]. July 23-29, 1939. P.

353. DIE NATION / IST ETWAS / GEWALTIGERES / ALS STAND, / HERKUNFT, / KLASSE / UND BERUF / ADOLF HITLER ["The nation is something mightier than rank, origin, class, and profession." Adolf Hitler]. July 30-Aug. 5, 1939. P.

354. UBER ALLER FREIHEIT DES / EINZELNEN STEHT DIE FREI-/HEIT UNSERES VOLKES / ADOLF HITLER ["Above all liberty of the individual stands the liberty of our nation." Adolf Hitler]. Aug. 13-19, 1939. P.

355. ES GIBT / KEINEN SOZIALISMUS, / DER NICHT AUFGEHT / IM / EIGENEN VOLK / ADOLF HITLER ["There is no socialism that is not absorbed by its own nation." Adolf Hitler]. Aug. 27-Sept. 2, 1939. P.

356. ICH GLAUBE / AN KEIN / RECHT IN / DER WELT, / DAS NICHT / VON EINER / MACHT BESCHIRMT IST. / ADOLF HITLER AM 30. JULI 1932 IN KEMPTEN ["I do not believe in any law in the world that is not protected by power." Adolf Hitler on 30 July, 1932, in Kempton]. Sept. 10-16, 1939. P.

357. GOTT GIBT / DIE NUSSE, / ABER ER / BEISST SIE / NICHT AUF. / GOETHE ["God gives us the nuts, but he does not crack them." Goethe]. Sept. 17-23, 1939. P.

358. WIR SIND / VERGANGLICH, / ABER / DEUTSCHLAND / MUSS LEBEN! / ADOLF HITLER ["We may perish, but Germany must live!" Adolf Hitler]. Sept. 24-30, 1939. P.

359. WEDER DAS DEUTSCHE / VOLK NOCH ICH / SIND AUF DEN VERTRAG / VON VERSAILLES VEREI-/DIGT

WORDEN, SONDERN / ICH BIN NUR VEREIDIGT / AUF DAS WOHL MEINES / VOLKES, DESSEN BEAUF-/TRAGTER ICH BIN. / ADOLF HITLER! ["Neither the German nation nor I were bound by oath to the Treaty of Versailles. Rather, I am bound by oath to the well-being of my people, whose representative I am." Adolf Hitler!]. June 30-July 6, 1940. P.

360. DER GEWINN / DES GESAMTOPFERS / WIRD DIE FREIHEIT / UND GROSSE UNSERES / VATERLANDES SEIN. / DR. GOEBBELS ["The reward of the common sacrifice shall be the freedom and greatness of our fatherland." Dr. Goebbels]. Aug. 25-31, 1940 (35th week). P.

361. DAS IST DIE / HOCHSTE RELIGION, / SEINEN ENKELN / EINEN / EHRLICHEN NAMEN, / EIN / FREIES LAND, / EINEN / STOLZEN SINN / ZU HINTERLASSEN. / ERNST MORITZ ARNDT ["This is the highest religion, to leave one's grandchildren an honest name, a free country, and a sense of pride." Ernst Moritz Arndt]. Sept. 1-7, 1940 (36th week). P.

362. DIE ZEIT IST EUER, / WAS SIE SEIN WIRD, / WIRD SIE DURCH / EUCH SEIN. CLAUSEWITZ ["The times are yours, what they will be, they will be through you." Clausewitz]. Sept. 8-14, 1940 (37th week). P.

363. HEROISMUS / IST NICHT NUR AUF DEM / SCHLACHTFELDE / NOTWEN-/DIG, SONDERN AUCH AUF / DEM BODEN DER HEIMAT / ADOLF HITLER ["Heroism is not only necessary on the battlefields but also on the soil of the homeland." Adolf Hitler]. Sept. 29-Oct. 5, 1940 (40th week). P.

364. DAS / BAUERNTUM / IST DER LEBENS-/QUELL / DES VOLKES / WALTHER DARRE / 1940 ["The peasantry is the lifeblood of the nation." Walther Darre, 1940]. Oct. 6-12, 1940 (41st week). P.

365. WER KLAGT / UND ZAGT-/TRAGT UNTER-/ GANGSGESICHT / WER LEBEN / WAGT, DER / STEIGT INS / SONNENLICHT / GEORG STAMMLER ["Whoever complains and hesitates represents defeat—Whoever dares life climbs up into the sunlight." Georg Stammler]. Oct. 13-19, 1940 (42nd week). P.

366. LIEBER / DAS LEBEN ALS / DIE TREUE / OPFERN [Better to sacrifice life than loyalty]. Oct. 20-26, 1940 (43rd week). P.

367. WER MIT / SEINEM / VOLK / NICHT / NOT UND TODTEILEN / WILL, DER IST NICHT / WERT, DASS ER MIT / IHM LEBE. JEAN PAUL ["Who is not prepared to share with his nation sacrifice and death does not deserve to live with it." Jean Paul]. Oct. 27-Nov. 2, 1940. P.

368. SIEGEN WIRD, / WER DEN / STARKEREN / GLAUBEN / BESITZT! [The victory belongs to those who have the stronger faith!] Nov. 3-9, 1940 (45th week). P.

369. STOLZ / AUF UNSERE / GROSSEN MANNER / DURFEN WIR NUR / SEIN SOLANGE SIE SICH / UNSERER NICHT / ZU SCHAMEN / BRAUCHEN. / V. CLAUSEWITZ ["We may be proud of our great men only as long as they do not need to be ashamed of us." V. Clausewitz]. Nov. 10-16, 1940 (46th week). P.

370. DES / FUHRERS / WORT / IST FUR UNS DEUTSCHE / BEFEHL [The word of the Fuhrer is for us Germans a command]. Nov. 24-30, 1940 (48th week). P.

371. DIE FUR DAS / VATERLAND STERBEN, / EHREN WIR AM BESTEN, / WENN WIR FUR DAS / VATERLAND LEBEN. / PETER ROSEGGER ["The best way to honor those who died for the fatherland is for us to live for the fatherland." Peter Rosegger]. Dec. 1-7, 1940 (49th week). P.

372. VON SCHIRACH / ALLES / GROSSE IN DER / WELT IST DURCH / TREUE GEWORDEN! [Von Schirach. "Everything great in the world has been accomplished through loyalty!"] Wittig-Friesen, artist. Dec. 8-14, 1940 (50th week). P.

373. AN DEN / FUHRER / GLAUBEN / HEISSTAN / DEN SIEG / GLAUBEN [To believe in the Fuhrer means to believe in victory]. Wittig-Friesen, artist. Dec. 15-21, 1940 (51st week). P.

374. DER / FUHRER / HANDELT, WENN DIE / ZEIT REIF IST! [The Fuhrer acts when the time is ripe!] Dec. 29, 1940-Jan. 4, 1941 (53rd week). P.

375. ES GIBT FALLE—WO / DAS HOCHSTE / WAGEN / DIE HOCHSTE WEIS-/HEIT IST. / CLAUSEWITZ ["There are

times when it is the greatest wisdom to take the greatest risks." Clausewitz]. Jan. 5-11, 1941 (2nd week). P.

376. ADOLF / HITLER / SAGT: ZU KAMPFEN / SIND WIR GEBOREN / DENN AUS DEM / KAMPF SIND WIR / GEKOMMEN! [Adolf Hitler says: "We are born to fight because we come from the fight!"] Wittig-Friesen, artist. Jan. 12-18, 1941 (3rd week). P.

377. DER FUHRER / SPRICHT: / UBER UNS ALLEN / STEHT DER GROSSE / BEFEHL: / DU MUSST IM DIENSTE / DEINES VOLKES DEINE / PFLICHT TUN! [The Fuhrer says: "Above all of us stands the great command: you must do your duty in the service of your nation!"] Jan. 19-25, 1941 (4th week). P.

378. OHNE BLUT / KEIN LEBEN, / OHNE OPFER / KEINE FREIHEIT! [Without blood, no life; without sacrifice, no liberty!] Feb. 2-8, 1941 (6th week). P.

379. SO WUNSCHENSWERT / EINE SCHNELLE ENTSCHEIDUNG / DES KRIEGES AUCH IST. / SO MUSS DOCH DIESEM ZWERK / NICHT DAS SCHICKSAL DES / KRIEGES GEOPFERT / ODER AUCH NUR IN / GEFAHR GESTELLT WERDEN. / GNEISENAU ["However desirable a quick determination of the war may be, we must not sacrifice the fate of war to this purpose nor even endanger it." Gneisenau]. Feb. 9-15, 1941 (7th week). P.

380. DER / FUHRER / HAT / IMMER / RECHT [The Fuhrer is always right]. Feb. 16-22, 1941 (8th week). P.

381. LICHT-LEBEN-KAMPF-SIEG / WAS KANN EINEM / VOLKE GESCHEHEN, / DESSEN JUGEND / AUF ALLES VERZICHTET, / UM SEINEM GROSSEN / IDEALE ZU DIENEN [Light-Life-Struggle-Victory. What can happen to a nation whose youth give up everything in order to serve their great ideal]. Wittig-Friesen, artist. Feb. 23-March 1, 1941 (9th week). P.

382. NUR / EINE STARKE REGIERUNG / KANN DEN FRIEDEN / VERBURGEN. / FRIEDLICHE VER-SICHERUNGEN / UNSERER NACHBARN SIND GE-/WISS SEHR WERTVOLL, ABER / SICHERHEIT FINDEN WIR /

NUR BEI UNS SELBST. / MOLTKE ["Only a strong government can insure peace. Peaceful assurances of our neighbors are certainly very valuable, but security is only found through ourselves." Moltke]. Hoyer, artist. March 2-8, 1941 (10th week). P.

383. GORING / KEINE / AUFGABE / IST SO GROSS, ALS / DASS SIE VON EINEM / DEUTSCHEN / NICHT GELOST WER-/DEN KONNTE! [Goring—"No task is so big that it could not be accomplished by a German!"] Wittig-Friesen, artist. March 9-15, 1941 (11th week). P.

384. OPFER SCHUFEN / DAS GROSS / DEUTSCHE / REICH DURCH / OPFER WIRD ES / EWIG SEIN! [Sacrifices created the great German Empire. Through sacrifices it will be made everlasting!] March 16-22, 1941 (12th week). P.

385. ADOLF / HITLER / EINES MUSS DIE WELT / ZUR KENNTNIS NEHMEN: / EINE NIEDERLAGE / DEUTSCHLANDS / WIRD EST NICHT GE-/BEN / WEDER MILITARISCH, NOCH / ZEITMASSIG, NOCH WIRT-/SCHAFTLICH [Adolf Hitler. "The world must recognize one thing: There will be no defeat of Germany, neither by military forces, nor by force of time, nor by economic forces"]. March 23-29, 1941 (13th week). P.

386. ADOLF HITLER / NICHT ETWA / DURCH VER-/TRAGE ODER / BUNDIGE AB-/MACHUNGEN, / SONDERN AUS-/SCHLIESSLICH / DURCH GEWALT, / HAT ENGLAND / SEIN RIESENHAF-/TES IMPERIUM / ZUSAMMEN GE-/ZIMMERT [Adolf Hitler. "Not by treaties or binding agreements but exclusively by force has England put together her enormous empire"]. Wittig-Friesen, artist. March 30-April 5, 1941 (14th week). P.

387. DEUTSCH-/LAND IST / WO TAPFE-/RE HERZEN / SIND. ULRICH / VON / HUTTEN ["Germany is where valiant hearts are." Ulrich von Hutten]. Wittig-Friesen, artist. April 6-12, 1941 (15th week). P.

388. WENN DIESER / KRIEG ABGESCHLOSSEN / SEIN WIRD, DANN SOLL IN / DEUTSCHLAND EIN GRO-/SSES SCHAFFEN BEGIN-/NEN, DANN WIRD EIN / GROSSES— WACHT AUF— / DURCH DIE DEUTSCHEN / LANDE ER-

TONEN. / ADOLF HITLER ["When this war has been terminated, then a great work will begin in Germany, a great 'Awake' will be heard throughout the German lands." Adolf Hitler]. Hoyer, artist. April 13-19, 1941 (16th week). P.

389. ZUM GEBURTSTAG / DES FUHRERS / DIE STARKE DER / STAATEN BERUHT / AUF DEN GROS-/SEN MANNERN / DIE IHNENZUR / RECHTEN STUNDE / GEBOREN / WERDEN / FRIEDRICH DER GROSSE [For the birthday of the Fuhrer—"The strength of the nations rests with the great men who are born to them at the right hour"—Frederick the Great]. Hoyer, artist. April 20-26, 1941 (17th week). P.

390. IN DIESEM / KRIEGE / SIEGT / NICHT / DAS GLUCK, / SONDERN / ENDLICH / EINMAL / DAS RECHT. / ADOLF HITLER ["In this war it is not luck that will triumph but, rather, justice that will finally prevail." Adolf Hitler]. May 11-17, 1941 (20th week). P.

391. ZUM MUTTERTAG: / "WAS DER MANN / EINSETZT AN HELDENMUT / AUF DEM SCHLACHTFELD, / SETZT DIE FRAU EIN IN EWIG / GEDULDIGER HINGABE, / IN EWIG GEDULDIGEM / LEIDEN UND ERTRAGEN" [For Mother's Day: "What the man gives in heroism on the battlefield, the woman gives in ever-patient devotion, in ever-patient suffering and endurance"]. Hoyer, artist. May 18-24, 1941 (21st week). P.

392. SEI, / WAS DU WILLST, / ABER WAS DU BIST, / HABE DEN MUT / GANZ ZU SEIN. / ALBERT LEO / SCHLAGETER ["Be what you want, but whatever you are, have the courage to be it completely." Albert Leo Schlageter]. May 25-31, 1941 (22nd week). P.

393. FRIEDRICH DER GROSSE / HELDEN / HABEN EUERE / REICH GESCHAF-/TEN. HALTET DIE-/SES REICH AUF-/RECHT, DAMIT DER / RUHM DER VA-/TER NICHT EURE / SCHANDE WIRD [Frederick the Great. "Heroes have created your empire. Preserve it in such a way that the glory of your fathers does not become your shame."]. Wittig-Friesen, artist. June 1-7, 1941 (23rd week). P.

394. DER WAHRE / SOZIALISMUS / ABER IST DIE / LEHRE VON DER / HARTESTEN / PFLICHT-/ERFULLUNG [True

socialism, however, is the doctrine of the hardest performance of duty]. Wittig-Friesen, artist. June 8-14, 1941 (24th week). P.

395. SICHERE / NERVEN / UND EISERNE / ZAHIGKEIT / SIND / DIE BESTEN / GARANTEN / FUR DIE / ERFOLGE / AUF DIESER / WELT / WORTE UNSERES FUHRERS ["Strong nerves and iron tenacity are the best guarantees for success in this world"—words of our Fuhrer]. Nov. 2-8, 1941 (45th week). P.

396. DIE NACHWELT / VERGISST DIE MANNER-/DIE NUR DEM EIGENEN / NUTZEN DIENTEN / UND RUHMT DIE HELDEN-/WELCHE AUF EIGENES / GLUCK VERZICHTETEN / WORTE DES FUHRERS ["Posterity forgets those who only served their own aims and praises the heroes who renounced their own happiness"—words of the Fuhrer]. Nov. 9-15, 1941 (46th week). P.

397. WAS / DIE FRONT / OPFERT, / DAS KANN / UBERHAUPT / DURCH NICHTS / VERGOLTEN / WERDEN / ADOLF / HITLER ["What the men at the front sacrifice cannot be repaid in any way at all." Adolf Hitler]. Dec. 7-13, 1941 (50th week). P.

398. WER DEN / MENSCHEN / WOHLTAT ERWEI-/SET—WIRD DAFUR / GESEGNET— / UND DAS IST / WAHRER / RUHM / FRIEDRICH-DER-GROSSE ["Whoever is kind to others will be blessed for it and that is true fame." Frederick the Great.]. Dec. 14-20, 1941 (51st week). P.

399. NATIONAL-/SOZIALISMUS / IST HOCHSTE / SOLDATISCHE / HALTUNG / IM GESAMTEN / LEBEN / HERMANN GORING ["National Socialism is highest soldierly bearing in all ways of life." Hermann Goring]. Jan.12-18, 1942 (3rd week). P.

400. FRIEDR. DER GROSSE / DES HELDEN HOHERE SEELE / MUSS DEM GROSSTEN-/WIE DEM KLEINSTEN AUCH IN / JEDER LAGE EIN BEISPIEL SEIN [Frederick the Great. "The greater soul of the hero must be an example to the highest and the lowest man in all situations"]. Jan. 19-25, 1942 (4th week). P.

401. OHNE DEN SIEG DES / HAKENKREUZES / GABE ES HEUTE KEINE / DEUTSCHE WEHR-/MACHT—SO

WENIG WIE / ES EINE DEUTSCHE / EHRE UND EINE / DEUTSCHE FREIHEIT / GABE / HERMANN GORING ["Without the victory of the swastika there would not be a German Army today and there would not be German honor or German freedom." Herman Goring]. Jan. 26-Feb. 1, 1942 (5th week). P.

402. AUS DEN "PFLICHTEN DES DEUTSCHEN SOLDATEN" / GROSSE LEISTUNGEN IN / KRIEG UND FRIEDEN ENT-/STEHEN NUR IN UNER-/SCHUTTERLICHER KAMPF-/GEMEINSCHAFT VON / FUHRER UND TRUPPE [From "The Duties of the German Soldier"—"Great achievements in war and peace can only be accomplished through an unshakable unity of Fuhrer and Army"]. Feb. 2-8, 1942 (6th week). P.

403. WENN DAS / VATERLAND / AUF DEM / SPIELE STEHT / GIBT ES FUR / NIEMANDEN / RECHTE, DA HAT / JEDERMANN / NUR / PFLICHTEN / WILDENBRUCH ["When the fatherland is at stake nobody has rights and privileges, everybody has only duties." Wildenbruch]. Feb. 9-15, 1942 (7th week). P.

404. WAS DIE HEIMAT LEISTET, / MUSS VOR DER GESCHICH-/TE DEREINST BESTEHEN / KONNEN / ADOLF HITLER ["What the homeland achieves must some day withstand the test of history." Adolf Hitler]. Knabe, artist. April 26-May 2, 1942 (18th week). P.

405. ADALBERT STIFTER / DAS / MUTTERHERZ / IST DER SCHONSTE UND / UNVERLIERBARSTE PLATZ / DES SOHNES, SELBST / WENN ER SCHON GRAUE / HAARE TRAGT,—UND JEDER / HAT IM GANZEN WELTALL / NUR EIN EINZIGES SOLCHES [Adalbert Stifter. "The heart of a mother is the most beautiful and the safest place for the son, even when his hair is already gray, and for everyone there is only one such place in the universe"]. Knabe, artist. May 17-23, 1942 (21st week). P.

406. ES GIBT KEINEN / BESSEREN DANK / FUR DEN EINSATZ UNSERER / SOLDATEN, ALS VOR ALLEM / MITZUHELFEN AN DER / HEILUNG IHRER WUNDEN / ADOLF HITLER ["There is no better way of thanking our soldiers for their courage than to help first of all to heal their

wounds." Adolf Hitler]. Knabe, artist. June 21-27, 1942 (26th week). P. (Fig. 38.)

407. SO WIE WIR / MITLEIDLOS / HART GEWE-/SEN SIND IM KAMPF / UM DIE MACHT, / WERDEN WIR GENAU / SO MITLEIDLOS UND / HART SEIN IM KAMPF UM / DIE ERHALTUNG / UNSERES VOLKES / ADOLF HITLER ["Hard and without pity as we have been in our struggle for power, so will we also be in the struggle for the preservation of our nation." Adolf Hitler]. July 26-Aug. 1, 1942 (31st week). P.

408. NUR DER / IST ZUR / KRITIK / BERECHTIGT, / DER EINE / AUFGABE / BESSER / LOSEN / KANN / ADOLF HITLER ["Only he has the right to criticize who can better solve the problem." Adolf Hitler]. Sept. 20-26, 1942 (39th week). P.

409. WIR / WOLLEN NICHT UNSEREN / KINDERN UND NACHKOMMEN / HINTERLASSEN WAS WIR SELBST / TUN KONNEN   HERMANN GORING ["We do not want to leave for our children and descendants what we can do ourselves." Hermann Goring]. Jan. 11-17, 1943 (3rd week). P. (Fig. 61.)

410. MEHR / TUN / ALS DIE / PFLICHT / BEFIEHLT! [Do more than duty demands!] Knabe, artist. Feb. 21-March 6, 1943 (9th and 10th weeks). P.

411. MOLTKE / WENN MAN / BEI EINEM GROSSEN / ENTSCHLUSS NICHT / ETWAS UBERS KNIE / BRICHT, NICHT EINIGE / RUCKSICHTEN UNBE-/RUCKSICHTIGT LASST, / SO KOMMT MAN IN DIE-/SEM LEBEN UM UND / NIMMER ZU ETWAS [Moltke—"When making a big decision those who cannot break some sticks, leave some considerations unconsidered, will never accomplish anything in this life and will perish"]. Wittig-Friesen, artist. May 10-16, 1943 (20th week). P.

412. MUTTER TAG / GOTT HAT DIE HERZEN / DER MUTTER GEWEIHT / ZU OPFERSCHALEN / DER GROSSEN ZEIT [Mother's Day—God has blessed the hearts of mothers as vessels of sacrifice in a time of greatness]. Knabe, artist. May 17-23, 1943 (21st week). P.

413. GEBEUGT / ERST / ZEIGT / DER BOGEN / SEINE / KRAFT / GRILLPARZER ["The bow shows its strength only

when bent." Grillparzer]. Ahrens, artist. May 31-June 6, 1943 (23rd week). P.

414. DER / NATIONAL / SOZIALISMUS / IST DER / GARANT / DES / SIEGES [National Socialism is the guarantor of victory]. P.

415. DER GLAUBE AN / DEN WERT DES BLUTES / UND AN DEN WERT DER / GERMANISCHEN RASSE / IST DIE VORAUSSETZUNG / DER NATIONALSOZIALISTI-/SCHEN WELTANSCHAU-/UNG. / A. ROSENBERG ["The belief in the value of blood and in the value of the Germanic race is the basis of the National Socialist doctrine." A. Rosenberg]. P.

GREAT BRITAIN

416. A BRITISH "BLENHEIM" BOMBER OF THE COASTAL COMMAND AIDS A BRITISH DESTROYER IN SMASHING A GERMAN SUBMARINE. Color. 38 x 51. Ak.

417. [Missing] FAMOUS BRITISH "SPITFIRES" FLYING IN FORMATION. EACH MACHINE CAN FIRE AT THE RATE OF OVER 6,000 CANNON AND / MACHINE GUN BULLETS PER MINUTE. James Gardner, artist. Color. 38 x 51. Ak.

418. GOING ASHORE? / BE CAREFUL TO WHOM YOU TALK AND WHAT YOU / . . . London: H.M.S.O. Color. 38 x 25. Ak.

419. H.M.S. "NELSON" FIRING A BROADSIDE WITH HER 16-INCH GUNS. THIS SHIP IS ARMED WITH / NINE OF THESE GREAT GUNS AND MANY SMALLER ONES. Color. 38 x 51. Ak.

420. HELP BRITAIN / FINISH THE JOB! Marc Stone, artist. London: H.M.S.O. Color. 76 x 51. Ak.

421. HELP BRITAIN / FINISH THE JOB! Wooton, artist. London: H.M.S.O. Color. 75 x 51. Ak.

422. LEADERS OF THE ALLIED NATIONS / WHOSE HEADQUARTERS / ARE IN BRITAIN. Color. 51 x 38. R. (Fig. 27.)

423. MUNITION WORKERS OF ALLIED COUNTRIES . . . / ARE HITTING BACK AT HITLER . . . / THROUGH BRITISH FACTORIES! Color. 50 x 38. R.

424. "NEVER WAS SO MUCH / OWED BY SO MANY / TO SO FEW" / THE PRIME MINISTER. London: H.M.S.O. Color. 76 x 51. Ak.

425. THE BRITISH COMMONWEALTH OF NATIONS / TOGETHER. London: H.M.S.O. Color. 101 x 150. Ak.

UNITED STATES

426. A CARELESS WORD . . . / A NEEDLESS LOSS. Anton Otto Fischer, artist. Washington: Office of War Information, no. 36, 1943. Color. 102 x 72. B. (Fig. 55.)

427. Same as 426. 71 x 56. Bl.

428. A CARELESS WORD . . . / . . . A NEEDLESS SINKING. Anton Otto Fischer, artist. Washington: Office of War Information, no. 24, 1942. Color. 71 x 56. B.

429. Same as 428. Bl.

430. A CARELESS WORD / . . . ANOTHER CROSS. John Atherton, artist. Washington: Office of War Information, no. 23, 1943. Color. 71 x 56. P.

431. Same as 430. B.

432. A LIFETIME EDUCATION FREE / FOR HIGH SCHOOL GRADUATES WHO QUALIFY / U. S. CADET NURSE CORPS / GO TO YOUR LOCAL HOSPITAL OR WRITE TO U. S. PUBLIC HEALTH SERVICE, BOX 88, NEW YORK 8, N. Y. Alex Ross, artist. Washington: Federal Security Agency, U. S. Public Health Service, 1945. Color. 67 x 47. R.

433. ALL FUEL IS SCARCE / PLAN FOR WINTER NOW! / THE SOLID FUELS ADMINISTRATION FOR WAR URGES: / 1 WINTERIZE YOUR HOME! / . . . / 2 CHECK YOUR

HEATING PLANT! / . . . / 3 ORDER FUEL AT ONCE! / . . . Albert Dorne, artist. Washington: Solid Fuels Administration for War, 1945. Color. 73 x 51. R.

434. AMERICANS SUFFER / WHEN CARELESS TALK KILLS! Harry Anderson, artist. Washington: GPO, 1943. Color. 51 x 36. R.

435. AMERICA'S ANSWER: / PRODUCTION. Jean Carlu, artist. Washington: Office For Emergency Management, 1942. Color. 77 x 103. Bl.

436. "—ANOTHER LARGE CONVOY / HAS ARRIVED SAFELY—" / BECAUSE / NO ONE / TALKED! 1942. Color. 58 x 42. R. (Fig. 56.)

437. ANOTHER TANKER TORPEDOED / OFF THE ATLANTIC COAST / SHOULD BRAVE MEN DIE / SO YOU CAN DRIVE . . . ? Washington: Office of Price Administration, 1942. Color. 51 x 72. R.

438. ANSWER THEIR / PRAYERS / AMERICAN RELIEF FOR HOLLAND / MEMBER AGENCY—NATIONAL WAR FUND. Douglass Crockwell, artist. Color. 56 x 36. H.

439. ATTACK   ATTACK   ATTACK / BUY WAR BONDS. Ferdinand Warren, artist. Washington: GPO, 1942. Color. 71 x 56. Bl.

440. AVENGE / DECEMBER 7. Bernard Perlin, artist. Washington: Office of War Information, no. 18, 1942. Color. 71 x 56.

441. AWARD / FOR CARELESS TALK / DON'T DISCUSS TROOP MOVEMENTS, SHIP SAILINGS, WAR EQUIPMENT. Stevan Dohanos, artist. Washington: Office of War Information, 1944. Color. 66 x 51. R.

442. BACK 'EM UP / BUY EXTRA BONDS. Boris Chaliapin, artist. Washington: U. S. Treasury Department. Color. 71 x 51. Ak.

443. BE A VICTORY FARM VOLUNTEER / IN THE U. S. CROP CORPS / SEE YOUR PRINCIPAL. Washington: U. S. Agriculture Department, 1943. Color. 56 x 36. R.

WW II: UNITED STATES

444. BE / GENEROUS / IN / VICTORY / GIVE / A VIRGINIAN'S SHARE / <u>YOUR</u> COMMUNITY WAR FUND. Color. 77 x 56. H. (Fig. 17.)

445. BECOME A NURSE / YOUR COUNTRY NEEDS YOU / WRITE NURSING INFORMATION BUREAU, 1790 BROADWAY, NEW YORK CITY. Washington: Office of War Information, no. 22, 1942. Color. 71 x 55. Ak.

446. BIG THINGS FROM LITTLE IDEAS GROW / THOMAS ALVA EDISON / AMERICA'S GREATEST INVENTOR / WORKED SMALL IDEAS / INTO BIG ONES / SPEED VICTORY / LET'S HAVE YOUR IDEAS. Washington: War Production Board, 1943. B & W. 108 x 72. R.

447. BOOKS CANNOT BE / KILLED BY FIRE. / PEOPLE DIE, BUT BOOKS NEVER DIE. / NO MAN AND NO FORCE CAN PUT / THOUGHT IN A CONCENTRATION CAMP / FOREVER. NO MAN AND NO FORCE CAN TAKE FROM THE WORLD THE BOOKS THAT / EMBODY MAN'S ETERNAL FIGHT AGAINST / TYRANNY. IN THIS WAR, WE KNOW, BOOKS / ARE WEAPONS. / FRANKLIN D. ROOSEVELT / BOOKS ARE WEAPONS IN THE WAR OF IDEAS. S. Broder, artist. Washington: Office of War Information, no. 7, 1942. Color. 71 x 51.

448. BOTTLENECKS / DELAY DELIVERY OF SUPPLIES / WASTE TRANSPORTATION SPACE / HOW CAN WE ELIMINATE THEM? / AWARDS / FOR YOUR IDEAS. Washington: Army Service Forces, suggestion poster no. 9, 1945. Color. 36 x 26. R.

449. BOWL THEM / OVER / MORE / PRODUCTION. Washington: War Production Board, 1942. Color. 103 x 73. Bl.

450. BUY NOW FOR THE / BIGGER 7TH / WAR LOAN / THROUGH PAYROLL SAVINGS. Washington: U. S. Treasury Department, 1945. Color. 71 x 51. R.

451. BUY WAR BONDS. Washington: GPO, 1942. Color. 136 x 103. Bl.

452. Same as 451. 71 x 51. Ak.

453. Same as 451. 36 x 28.

454. ... / BUY WAR BONDS / MORE TOMAHAWKS / FOR OUR UNITED WARRIORS / BUY WAR BONDS NOW! / I / NEED / YOUR / HELP / ... Eah-Ha-Wa and Hå å tee Ben, artists. Washington: U. S. Treasury Department, 1942. Color. 97 x 61. Bl.

455. CALLING / ALL ROOMS! / 1000 NEW WAR / DEPT. EMPLOYES / ARE COMING / AND WILL NEED / ROOMS! / HAVE YOU A ROOM TO RENT OR SHARE? / KNOW OF ONE THAT WILL BE VACANT? / CALL 2973. Washington: U.S. War Department, Housing Center. Color. 51 x 36. R.

456. CARELESS MATCHES AID THE AXIS / PREVENT FOREST FIRES! Washington: U. S. Agriculture Department, U. S. Forest Service, 1942. Color. 24 x 18. R.

457. CARELESS TALK / <u>GOT THERE FIRST</u>. Ray Prohaska, artist. Washington: GPO, 1944. Color. 71 x 51.

458. CARELESS TALK / ... GOT THERE FIRST. Washington: GPO, 1944. Color. 71 x 51. PL.

459. CHINA / FIGHTS ON / UNITED CHINA RELIEF / MEMBER AGENCY OF THE NATIONAL WAR FUND. Gaydos, artist. Color. 56 x 36. H.

460. CHINA FIRST TO / FIGHT! / UNITED CHINA RELIEF / PARTICIPATING IN NATIONAL WAR FUND. Martha Sawyers, artist. Color. 104 x 69. R.

461. CHINA / SHALL HAVE / OUR HELP! / UNITED CHINA RELIEF. Martha Sawyers, artist. Color. 104 x 69. P.

462. CONSTANT / COMPANIONS / AMBITION—SUCCESS / BE AMBITIOUS AND SEND IN / A SUGGESTION EVERY WEEK! Washington: Army Service Forces, suggestion poster no. 10. Color. 34 x 25. R.

463. COST OF LIVING / IN TWO WARS / KEEP UP THE GOOD WORK / KEEP DOWN LIVING COSTS / PAY NO MORE THAN CEILING PRICES. Leon Helguera, artist. Washington: GPO, 1944. Color. 71 x 51. R.

464. COULD THIS BE YOU? / DON'T TRAVEL—UNLESS / YOUR TRIP HELPS WIN THE WAR. Washington: Office of Defense Transportation, 1945. Color. 66 x 47. R.

465. COURAGE AND GALLANTRY IN ACTION / INFANTRY / UNITED STATES ARMY. Jes Wilhelm Schlaikjer, artist. Washington: U. S. War Department, 1943. Color. 64 x 31. R. (Fig. 57.)

466. "DELIVER US FROM EVIL" / BUY WAR BONDS. Washington: U. S. Treasury Department, 1943. Color. 36 x 27.

467. DO WITH LESS— / SO THEY'LL HAVE / ENOUGH! / RATIONING GIVES YOU YOUR FAIR SHARE. Washington: Office of War Information, no. 37, 1943. Color. 102 x 73. Bl.

468. Same as 467. 71 x 56. Bl.

469. DO YOUR PART JOIN THE WAAC / WOMEN'S ARMY AUXILIARY CORPS / UNITED STATES ARMY / APPLY AT ANY U. S. ARMY RECRUITING AND INDUCTION STATION. Washington: U. S. Army, Recruiting Publicity Bureau, 1942. Color. 98 x 64. R.

470. DO YOUR PART TO WIN THE WAR / BUY MORE WAR SAVINGS STAMPS / . . . . Washington: U. S. Treasury Department, 1942. Color. 56 x 71. Bl.

471. DOC SALVAGE SAYS— / DON'T MIX YOUR CHIPS! / . . . YOUR SCRAP CAN FIGHT—IF YOU SORT IT RIGHT! / . . . Washington: U.S. Navy, Industrial Incentive Division. Color. 77 x 112. R.

472. DOCTORS ARE SCARCE / ONE OUT OF THREE HAS GONE TO WAR / BE PREPARED / FOR MINOR INJURY / FOR MINOR ILLNESS / LEARN FIRST AID / & HOME NURSING. Washington: Office of War Information, no. 27, 1943. Color. 71 x 56. R.

473. "DOING ALL YOU CAN, BROTHER?" / BUY WAR BONDS. Robert Sloan, artist. Washington: GPO, 1943. Color. 103 x 73. Bl.

474. Same as 473. 71 x 56. Bl.

475. DON'T BE / CAPTURED / BY / VENEREAL / DISEASE. F. Williams, artist. Color. 36 x 28. P.

476. DON'T LET THAT SHADOW TOUCH THEM / BUY WAR BONDS. Lawrence Smith, artist. Washington: GPO, 1942. Color. 51 x 37. Bl.

477. DON'T LET THIS BUG / GET YOU! / ABSENTEEISM / YOUR / LABOR MANAGEMENT COMMITTEE. Washington: War Production Board, 1943. Color. 54 x 34. R.

478. DON'T LET THIS HAPPEN TO YOU! / ORDER COAL NOW! Fitzpatrick, artist. Washington: Solid Fuels Administration for War, 1944. Color. 71 x 51. R.

479. DON'T SHIVER / NEXT WINTER . . . / ORDER COAL / NOW! Arens, artist. Washington: Solid Fuels Administration for War, 1944. Color. 66 x 47. R.

480. 85 / MILLION / AMERICANS / HOLD / WAR BONDS. Washington: U. S. Treasury Department, 1945. Color. 36 x 26. R.

481. ENLIST IN A PROUD PROFESSION! / JOIN THE / U. S. CADET NURSE CORPS / A LIFETIME EDUCATION— / FREE! / IF YOU CAN QUALIFY / FOR INFORMATION / GO TO YOUR LOCAL HOSPITAL / OR WRITE U. S. CADET NURSE CORPS, BOX 88, NEW YORK, N. Y. Edmundson, artist. Washington: Federal Security Agency, U. S. Public Health Service. Color. 71 x 51. R.

482. ENLIST IN A PROUD PROFESSION . . . / JOIN THE / U. S. / CADET / NURSE / CORPS / A LIFETIME EDUCATION / FREE! / FOR HIGH SCHOOL / GRADUATES WHO QUALIFY / FOR INFORMATION GO TO YOUR LOCAL HOSPITAL OR WRITE / U. S. CADET NURSE CORPS, BOX 88, NEW YORK, N. Y. Washington: Federal Security Agency, U. S. Public Health Service, 1943. Color. 71 x 51. R.

483. "EVEN A LITTLE / CAN HELP A LOT—NOW" / BUY / U. S. WAR STAMPS BONDS. A. Parker, artist. Washington: GPO, 1942. Color. 51 x 36. Bl.

484. "EVERY JOB IS A FIGHTING MAN'S / JOB. MINUTES COUNT WITH FREE-/DOM AT STAKE. LET'S CRAM THEM / FULL OF WORK!" / PRODUCE FOR VICTORY! Chicago: The Sheldon-Claire Co., 1942. Color. 91 x 61. R.

485. EXHIBITION / U. S. ARMY / HOSPITAL TRAIN / FOR USE IN / COMBAT AREAS / FULLY STAFFED AND EQUIPPED! / ... / ONE DAY ONLY / WEDNESDAY, NOVEMBER 24 / 1-9 P.M., TRACK NO. 4 / BROAD STREET STATION / PHILADELPHIA / PENNSYLVANIA RAILROAD / BUY U. S. WAR BONDS AND STAMPS. Color. 103 x 64. R.

486. FARMERS! / UNCLE SAM ASKS YOU ... / TO GET READY FOR THE CENSUS TAKER / IN JANUARY THE U. S. CENSUS BUREAU WILL ASK / YOU ABOUT 1944 CROPS ... / THE LAW REQUIRING YOUR REPORTS MAKES THEM CONFIDENTIAL. Jerome Rozen, artist. Washington: U.S. Commerce Department, Bureau of the Census, 1944. Color. 68 x 48. R.

487. FILL IT! / HELP HARVEST WAR CROPS / SEE YOUR COUNTY EXTENSION AGENT OR LOCAL FARM EMPLOYMENT OFFICE. Stevan Dohanos, artist. Washington: War Food Administration, 1945. Color. 72 x 56. R.

488. FOLLOW ME! MEN 18-19 / ... / APPLY NOW AT ANY / U.S. ARMY / RECRUITING AND INDUCTION STATION / ... Washington: U.S. Army, Recruiting Publicity Bureau, 1942. Color. 97 x 65. R.

489. "FOR ALL THAT CARELESS / TALK—THANKS!" / ADOLPH / ARE YOU BUCKING FOR / THE IRON CROSS? Dick Wiley, artist. San Francisco: Headquarters, Western Defense Command and Fourth Army, 1943. Color. 39 x 29. P.

490. FOR DEFENSE / BUY / UNITED / STATES / SAVINGS / BONDS / AND STAMPS / ASK ABOUT OUR PAYROLL ALLOTMENT PLAN. Washington: GPO, 1941. Color. 34 x 25. Bl.

491. FOR FREEDOM'S / SAKE / BUY WAR BONDS. Washington: GPO, 1943. Color. 36 x 28. Bl.

492. FOR HEALTH ... EAT SOME FOOD / FROM EACH GROUP ... EVERY DAY! / ... / IN ADDITION TO THE BASIC 7 ... / EAT ANY OTHER FOODS YOU WANT. Washington: U. S. Department of Agriculture, 1943. Color. 71 x 56. Bl.

493. FOR THEIR / FUTURE— / BUY WAR BONDS. Munsett, artist. Washington: GPO, 1943. Color. 71 x 56. Bl.

494. FOR WAR SERVICE / SEEING IT THROUGH / ARE YOU? Washington: U. S. Army, 1945. Color. 76 x 54. R.

495. Same as 494. 36 x 26. R.

496. FUEL / FIGHTS / SAVE YOUR SHARE / . . . . Washington: GPO, 1943. Color. 71 x 51. R.

497. GET A WAR JOB / TO HELP HIM FIGHT / SEE NEAREST U. S. EMPLOYMENT SERVICE. Washington: GPO, 1942. Color. 69 x 50. Bl.

498. GET YOUR FARM IN THE FIGHT! / USE CONSERVATION METHODS / FOR BIGGER YIELDS NOW! / FOOD / FOR FREEDOM. Washington: GPO, 1942. Color. 71 x 48. R. (Fig. 46.)

499. "GIVE 'EM THE STUFF / TO FIGHT WITH . . . ." Sarra, artist. Washington: Office of Facts and Figures, Graphics Division, 1942. Color. 55 x 41. R.

500. "GIVE 'EM THE STUFF / TO FIGHT WITH . . . " / FIGHT FOR FREEDOM! John Falter, artist. Washington: Office of Facts and Figures, Graphics Division, 1942. Color. 26 x 18. R.

501. GIVE IT YOUR BEST! Washington: Office of War Information, no. 9, 1942. Color. 51 x 72. Bl.

502. Same as 501. By.

503. GIVE TO YOUR / WAR FUND / FOR OUR OWN— / FOR OUR ALLIES. National War Fund. Color. 72 x 52. R.

504. GOOD NEWS FROM HOME / TANKS / PLANES / GUNS / SHIPS / MORE PRODUCTION. Stevan Dohanos, artist. Washington: War Production Board, 1942. Color. 103 x 73. Bl.

505. GROW YOUR OWN / BE SURE! / GARDEN / IN / 1945 / FOR / VICTORY. Grover Strong, artist. Color. 58 x 41. R.

506. HAVE YOU / REALLY TRIED / TO SAVE GAS / BY GETTING INTO / A CAR CLUB? Harold von Schmidt, artist. Washington: GPO, 1944. Color. 71 x 52. R.

507. HELP BRING THEM BACK TO YOU! / FIND TIME FOR WAR / WORK / RAISE AND SHARE / FOOD / . . . MAKE YOURS / A VICTORY HOME! Washington: Office of War Information, no.41, 1943. Color. 71 x 56. Bl.

508. HERE'S HOW TO HEAD OFF / RUNAWAY PRICES / FOLLOW THE 7-KEY PLAN TO / HOLD PRICES DOWN / V / I / C / T / O / R / Y. Color. 57 x 42. R.

509. HE'S A "FIGHTING / FOOL"— / GIVE / HIM THE BEST / YOU'VE GOT! / MORE PRODUCTION. Noxon, artist. Washington: War Production Board, 1942. Color. 102 x 72. R.

510. HE'S FIGHTING FOR YOU / JOIN THE STAMP CLUB / A STAMP A DAY / . . . FOR THE MAN / WHO'S AWAY . . . Washington: GPO, 1943. Color. 71 x 56. Bl.

511. HOLDING THE LINE! Henri Guignon, artist. Color. 53 x 35. Ak.

512. HOME FRONT FIRES / ARE ENEMY / VICTORIES / PREVENT FIRES. Jes Wilhelm Schlaikjer, artist. Washington: GPO, 1944. Color. 71 x 51. R.

513. "I AM LOOKING FORWARD TO DICTATING / PEACE TO THE UNITED STATES IN THE / WHITE HOUSE AT WASHINGTON" / ADMIRAL YAMAMOTO / WHAT DO YOU SAY, AMERICA? Washington: Office of War Information, Graphics Division, 1942. Color. 51 x 35. R.

514. I NEED YOU ON THE JOB FULL TIME . . . / DON'T GET HURT. Nancy Morse Meyers, artist. Washington: War Department Safety Council, 1943. Color. 101 x 72.

515. I NEED YOUR SKILL / IN A WAR JOB! / IF YOU KNOW ONE OF THESE TRADES AND ARE NOT / NOW IN REAL WAR WORK, YOU ARE BADLY NEEDED / . . . / SEE YOUR NEAREST U. S. EMPLOYMENT SERVICE. James Montgomery Flagg, artist. Washington: Office of War Information, no. 25, 1943. Color. 71 x 56. R.

516. I WANT YOU / FOR THE U. S. ARMY / ENLIST NOW. James Montgomery Flagg, artist. Washington: U.S. Army, Recruiting Publicity Bureau, 1940. Color. 96 x 64. R. (Fig. 2.)

517. IF YOU TELL WHERE / HE'S GOING . . . HE MAY NEVER / GET THERE! John Falter, artist. Washington: Office of War Information, 1943. Color. 71 x 51.

518. IF YOU TELL / WHERE YOU'RE GOING . . . / YOU MAY / NEVER GET THERE / DON'T TALK ABOUT TROOP MOVEMENTS. Washington: U. S. War Department, Adjutant General's Office, 1943. Color. 71 x 56. P.

519. I'LL CARRY MINE TOO! / TRUCKS AND TIRES MUST LAST TILL VICTORY. Sarra, artist. Washington: Office of War Information, no. 28, 1943. Color. 71 x 56. Bl.

520. I'M COUNTING ON YOU! / DON'T DISCUSS: / TROOP MOVEMENTS / SHIP SAILINGS • WAR EQUIPMENT. Washington: Office of War Information, no. 78, 1943. Color. 19 x 24. R.

521. IN LOYAL SUPPORT / OF OUR FIGHTING MEN, WE HAVE / PLEDGED OURSELVES TO REMIND / EVERY AMERICAN TO BUY MORE / WAR STAMPS & BONDS NOW. Washington: GPO, 1943. Color. 36 x 28. Bl.

522. IN MEMORY / U.S.S. "DORADO" / FIRE AWAY! / BUY EXTRA BONDS / 5TH V-WAR LOAN. Georges Schreiber, artist. Washington: U. S. Treasury Department, War Finance Division, 1944. Color. 71 x 51. R.

523. Same as 522. Ak.

524. IN THE FACE OF OBSTACLES—COURAGE / INFANTRY / UNITED STATES ARMY. Jes Wilhelm Schlaikjer, artist. Washington: U. S. War Department, 1943. Color. 84 x 84. R.

525. INVENT FOR / VICTORY / ALL AMERICANS WHO HAVE AN INVENTION / OR AN IDEA WHICH MIGHT BE USEFUL TO / THEIR COUNTRY ARE URGED TO SEND IT / IMMEDIATELY TO / NATIONAL INVENTIONS COUNCIL / DEPARTMENT OF COMMERCE— WASHINGTON, D. C. Elmo White, artist. Washington: U. S. Department of Commerce. Color. 71 x 51.

526. IT IS GOOD TO HEAR / AMERICANS ARE NOW PUDDING / 10% OF DER PAY INTO BUNDS! / HERMAN, / YOU TELL HIM / IT ISS BONDS— / NOT BUNDS! / FOR

VICTORY . . . PUT AT LEAST 10% / OF EVERY PAY INTO WAR BONDS! Washington: U.S. Treasury Department, War Savings Staff, 1942. Color. 56 x 43.

527. IT'LL BE A GREAT DAY! / CONSERVATION / OF SUPPLIES AND EQUIPMENT / SPEEDS VICTORY. Harold von Schmidt, artist. Washington: U. S. Army Conservation Program, 1944. Color. 52 x 32. R.

528. JUST BE SURE / YOU PUT AT LEAST / 10% OF IT IN / WAR BONDS! / TOP THAT 10%. Washington: U. S. Treasury Department, War Savings Staff, 1942. Color. 71 x 56. R.

529. JUST BY / KEEPING WELL / YOU CAN HELP WIN THIS WAR / . . . / FOLLOW / THESE / 5 / SIMPLE / HEALTH / RULES. Color. 51 x 35. Bl.

530. KEEP HIM FLYING! / BUY WAR BONDS. Georges Schrieber, artist. Washington: U. S. Treasury Department, War Savings Staff, 1943. Color. 71 x 56.

531. KEEP THE ENEMY / IN THE DARK! / BE CAREFUL— / WHAT YOU SAY . . OR WRITE! Washington: U. S. War Department, Adjutant General's Office. Color. 53 x 36.

532. KEEP THE / HOME FRONT PLEDGE / PAY NO MORE THAN CEILING / PRICES / PAY YOUR POINTS IN FULL. Washington: GPO, 1944. Color. 71 x 51.

533. KEEP US FLYING / BUY WAR BONDS. Washington: U. S. Treasury Department, War Finance Division, 1943. Color. 71 x 51. R.

534. KINDA GIVE IT YOUR / PERSONAL ATTENTION, WILL YOU? / MORE PRODUCTION. Rolse, artist. Washington: War Production Board. Color. 103 x 71. Bl.

535. LESS DANGEROUS / THAN CARELESS TALK / DON'T DISCUSS TROOP MOVEMENTS—SHIP SAILINGS—WAR EQUIPMENT. Albert Dorne, artist. Washington: Office of War Information, 1944. Color. 72 x 51. R. (Fig. 25.)

536. LET 'EM HAVE IT / BUY / EXTRA BONDS. Bernard Perlin, artist. Washington: U. S. Treasury Department, War Finance Division, 1943. Color. 100 x 72. By.

WW II: UNITED STATES

537. Same as 536. R.

538. Same as 536. 71 x 51. H.

539. LET'S / ALL / FIGHT / BUY WAR BONDS. Washington: GPO, 1942. Color. 56 x 71. Bl.

540. Same as 539. 28 x 36. Bl.

541. LET'S FINISH THE JOB! / URGENT— / EXPERIENCED SEAMEN NEEDED! / WIRE COLLECT: MERCHANT MARINE, WASHINGTON, D. C. / OR INQUIRE YOUR MARITIME UNION OR U. S. EMPLOYMENT SERVICE. Martha Sawyers, artist. Washington: U. S. Merchant Marine, 1944. Color. 71 x 51. R.

542. LET'S GIVE HIM / ENOUGH AND ON TIME. Norman Rockwell, artist. Washington: U. S. Army, Ordnance Department, 1942. Color. 73 x 102. R.

543. LET'S / TEAM UP / TO KEEP FOOD PRICES DOWN / FOR THE SAKE OF / AMERICA'S FUTURE. Washington: Office of Price Administration, 1944. Color. 71 x 50. R.

544. LEXINGTON, 1775 / . . . / INDEPENDENCE, JULY 4, 1776 / . . . / JOHN PAUL JONES SAID: / 'I HAVE NOT YET BEGUN TO / FIGHT' / . . . / WASHINGTON CROSSED THE / DELAWARE /. . . . J. Daugherty, artist. Washington: GPO, 1942. Color. 98 x 64. Bl.

545. MAKE YOUR OWN / DECLARATION OF WAR / . . . / BUY WAR BONDS. Washington: GPO, 1942. Color. 71 x 56. Bl.

546. MATCH THEIR COURAGE / WITH YOUR / RESPONSIBILITY / OVERSEAS / SHIPMENTS / MUST BE / MARKED RIGHT / THE ARMY MARKING / SYSTEM IS EASY TO / APPLY IF YOU FOLLOW / INSTRUCTIONS / IF YOU DON'T KNOW / ASK THE BOSS. . . . Jes Wilhelm Schlaikjer, artist. Washington: U. S. War Department, 1943. Color. 86 x 107. R.

547. ME TRAVEL? / . . . NOT THIS SUMMER / VACATION AT HOME / OFFICE OF DEFENSE TRANSPORTATION. Albert Dorne, artist. Washington: Office of Defense Transportation, 1945. Color. 66 x 48. R. (Fig. 47.)

548. MEN OF 18 AND 19 / NOW YOU CAN CHOOSE / YOUR BRANCH OF SERVICE / APPLY AT THE NEAREST U. S. ARMY RECRUITING AND INDUCTION STATION. Washington: U. S. Army Recruiting Publicity Bureau, 1942. Color. 97 x 65. R.

549. MILITARY GOVERNMENT—GERMANY / SUPREME COMMANDER'S AREA OF CONTROL / PROCLAMATION NO. 1 / TO THE PEOPLE OF GERMANY: / I, GENERAL DWIGHT D. EISENHOWER, SUPREME COMMANDER, ALLIED EXPEDITIONARY FORCE, DO HEREBY PROCLAIM AS FOLLOWS:— / . . . B & W. 51 x 53. P. (Fig. 1.)

550. MINE AMERICA'S COAL / ". . . WE'LL MAKE IT HOT / FOR THE ENEMY!" / SEE YOUR UNITED STATES EMPLOYMENT SERVICE / WAR MANPOWER COMMISSION. Norman Rockwell, artist. Washington: U. S. Employment Service, War Manpower Commission, 1944. Color. 51 x 36. R.

551. MINE EYES HAVE SEEN THE GLORY / WOMEN'S ARMY CORPS / ARMY OF THE UNITED STATES. Jes Wilhelm Schlaikjer, artist. Washington: U. S. War Department, 1944. Color. 64 x 39. R.

552. MORE AMERICAN WORKERS WERE KILLED AND WOUNDED IN / INDUSTRIAL ACCIDENTS LAST YEAR THAN ALL THE CASUALTIES / FROM BOMBS IN BRITAIN IN TWO YEARS OF WAR / FOLLOW SAFETY RULES! Washington: War Production Board, 1942. Color. 102 x 73. R. (Fig. 22.)

553. MORE / PRODUCTION. Washington: War Production Board, 1942. Color. 26 x 18. R.

554. "MOSQUITOES" / . . . DASHING THROUGH THE / SEAS AT EXPRESS TRAIN / SPEED, THE NAVY'S P-T / BOATS PROTECT OUR SHORES / AND PACK A STING . . . / ENLIST TODAY / THE UNITED STATES NAVY. U. S. Navy, 1941. Color. 36 x 43. Bl.

555. NEW YEAR / SUGGESTION / AT / LEAST / ONE / GOOD / SUGGESTION / THIS / YEAR. C. X. Carlson, artist.

Washington: U. S. War Department, suggestion poster no. 15, 1944. Color. 33 x 23. R.

556. NEW ZEALAND / FIGHTS. Color. 81 x 61. R.

557. NEW ZEALAND FIGHTS / IN PACIFIC SKIES. Washington: The New Zealand Legation. Color. 62 x 82. R.

558. NEXT! / JAPAN / 6TH / WAR / LOAN. Bingham, artist. Washington: U. S. Treasury Department, War Finance Division, 1944. Color. 71 x 51. R.

559. NOW IS THE TIME! / APPLY AT THE NEAREST / U. S. ARMY / RECRUITING AND INDUCTION STATION. Washington: U. S. Army, Recruiting Publicity Bureau, 1942. Color. 97 x 65. R.

560. O'ER THE RAMPARTS WE WATCH / UNITED STATES / ARMY AIR FORCE. Jes Wilhelm Schlaikjer, artist. Washington: U. S. War Department, 1944. Color. 64 x 39. R.

561. "OF COURSE I CAN! / I'M PATRIOTIC AS CAN BE— / AND RATION POINTS WON'T WORRY ME!" Dick Williams, artist. Washington: War Food Administration, 1944. Color. 65 x 47. R.

562. OF THE TROOPS / AND FOR THE TROOPS / THE CORPS OF / MILITARY POLICE / UNITED STATES ARMY. Jes Wilhelm Schlaikjer, artist. Washington: U. S. War Department, Bureau of Public Relations, 1942. Color. 64 x 31. R.

563. OUR CARELESSNESS / THEIR SECRET WEAPON / PREVENT FOREST FIRES. Washington: U. S. Agriculture Department, U. S. Forest Service, 1943. Color. 71 x 56. H.

564. OUR FIGHTERS / DESERVE OUR BEST. Washington: U. S. Army Ordnance Department, 1942. Color. 103 x 73. Bl.

565. OURS . . . TO FIGHT FOR / FREEDOM FROM FEAR. Norman Rockwell, artist. Washington: Office of War Information, no. 46, 1943. Color. 71 x 51. M.

566. OURS . . . TO FIGHT FOR / FREEDOM FROM WANT. Norman Rockwell, artist. Washington: Office of War Information, no. 45, 1943. Color. 71 x 51. M.

567. Same as 566. By.

568. OURS... TO FIGHT FOR / FREEDOM OF SPEECH FREEDOM OF WORSHIP / FREEDOM FROM WANT FREEDOM FROM FEAR. Norman Rockwell, artist. Washington: Office of War Information, no. 47, 1943. Color. 103 x 73. Bl.

569. PLANT A VICTORY GARDEN / OUR FOOD / IS FIGHTING / A GARDEN WILL MAKE YOUR RATIONS GO FURTHER. Washington: Office of War Information, no. 34, 1943. Color. 71 x 56. R.

570. Same as 569. Bl.

571. PLENTY TOUGH / BECAUSE HE EATS PLENTY / YOUR RATION STAMPS HELP KEEP HIM THAT WAY / SAYS MAJOR GENERAL E. B. GREGORY QUARTERMASTER GENERAL U. S. ARMY. Chicago: Pillsbury Flour Mills Company. Color. 67 x 50. R.

572. POLISH WAR RELIEF / OF THE U.S.A., INC. / FOR THE POOR AND THE FATHERLESS / POLISH WAR RELIEF OF U.S.A., INC.—MEMBER AGENCY OF NATIONAL WAR FUND, INC. W. T. Bendix, artist. Color. 56 x 35. H. (Fig. 54.)

573. PREPARE FOR YOUR WAR JOB NOW! / MILLIONS ARE NEEDED—SHORT FREE COURSES / IF YOU ARE... / WHAT TO DO... / APPLY... Washington: War Manpower Commission, 1943. Color. 54 x 112. R.

574. PVT. JOE LOUIS SAYS— / "WE'RE GOING TO DO OUR PART / ... AND WE'LL WIN BECAUSE / WE'RE ON GOD'S SIDE." Washington: Office of Facts and Figures, Graphics Division, 1942. Color. 51 x 36. R. (Fig. 5.)

575. PROTECT / HIS / FUTURE / BUY AND KEEP WAR BONDS. Ruth Nichols, artist. Washington: U. S. Treasury Department, War Finance Division, 1944. Color. 71 x 51. R.

576. Same as 575. 36 x 26. R.

577. RADIOGRAM / TO MEN OF 18 AND 19 / NEW ENLISTMENT PRIVILEGES / ... / APPLY NOW AT ANY U. S. ARMY RECRUITING & INDUCTION STATION. Washington: U. S. Army, Recruiting Publicity Bureau, 1942. Color. 97 x 65. R.

578. REACH YOUR BOY / OVERSEAS / BY / V-MAIL / THE LETTERS / THAT TRAVEL ON FILM / EASY TO USE / SUREST- / FASTEST- / AND MOST / PATRIOTIC / YOUR STATIONER AND POST OFFICE HAVE / V-MAIL LETTER FORMS. Jes Wilhelm Schlaikjer, artist. Washington: GPO, 1942. Color. 71 x 56. R.

579. RIGHT / IS / MIGHT / U. S. ARMY / MEN 18-19 / . . . CHOOSE NOW! / APPLY AT ANY U. S. ARMY RECRUITING AND INDUCTION STATION. Stu Graves, artist. Washington: U. S. Army, Recruiting Publicity Bureau, 1942. Color. 97 x 65. R. (Fig. 52.)

580. SAFE WORK SPEEDS VICTORY. Washington: U. S. Army, Ordnance Department, 1942. Color. 33 x 618 [Banner]. R.

581. SAVE FREEDOM OF SPEECH / BUY WAR BONDS. Norman Rockwell, artist. Washington: Office of War Information, no. 44, 1943. Color. 71 x 51. M.

582. SAVE FREEDOM OF WORSHIP / BUY WAR BONDS. Norman Rockwell, artist. Washington: Office of War Information, no. 43, 1943. Color. 71 x 51. M.

583. SAVE HIS LIFE . . . / AND FIND / YOUR OWN / BE A NURSE / WRITE TO STUDENT NURSES, 1790 BROADWAY, N.Y.C. Washington: Office of War Information, no. 49, 1943. Color. 56 x 36. Bl.

584. SAVE WASTE FATS FOR EXPLOSIVES / TAKE THEM TO YOUR MEAT DEALER. H. Koerner, artist. Washington: Office of War Information, no. 63, 1943. Color. 58 x 41. R. (Fig. 48.)

585. SAVE YOUR CANS / HELP PASS THE AMMUNITION / PREPARE YOUR TIN CANS / FOR WAR / . . . McClelland Barclay, artist. Washington: War Production Board, Salvage Division. Color. 85 x 64. R.

586. SERVICE ABOVE SELF / MEDICAL DEPARTMENT / UNITED STATES ARMY. Jes Wilhelm Schlaikjer, artist. Washington: U. S. War Department, Bureau of Public Relations, 1942. Color. 64 x 39. R.

587. 1778-1943 / AMERICANS / WILL ALWAYS FIGHT FIGHT FOR LIBERTY. Bernard Perlin, artist. Washington: Office of War Information, no. 26, 1943. Color. 103 x 73. Bl.

588. Same as 587. 71 x 56. Bl.

589. 7TH / WAR LOAN NOW—ALL TOGETHER. C. C. Beall, artist. Washington: U. S. Treasury Department, War Finance Division, 1945. Color. 94 x 66. R. (Fig. 21.)

590. Same as 589. 47 x 66. Ba.

591. Same as 589. 47 x 66. Re.

592. Same as 589. 33 x 23. R.

593. SHE'S A SWELL PLANE- / GIVE US MORE! / MORE PRODUCTION. Riggs, artist. Washington: War Production Board. Color. 103 x 71. Bl.

594. SILENCE— / —MEANS SECURITY / BE CAREFUL WHAT YOU / SAY OR WRITE. Jes Wilhelm Schlaikjer, artist. Washington: U. S. War Department, 1945. Color. 52 x 38. R.

595. SOLDIER'S LIFE / MAKE THE / REGULAR / ARMY / YOUR / CAREER. Tom B. Woodburn, artist. Washington: U. S. Army, Recruiting Publicity Bureau, 1941. Color. 96 x 65. R.

596. SOMEBODY BLABBED / DON'T TALK ABOUT SHIP MOVEMENTS! / DON'T TALK ABOUT WAR PRODUCTION! / BUTTON YOUR LIP! Albert Dorne, artist. Washington: Office of Facts and Figures, Graphics Division, 1942. Color. 26 x 18. R.

597. SOMEONE TALKED! Siebel, artist. Washington: Office of War Information, no. 18, 1942. Color. 102 x 72. R.

598. Same as 597. B.

599. Same as 597. Bl.

600. STAMP OUT / BLACK MARKETS / . . . WITH YOUR RATION STAMPS / PAY NO MORE THAN LEGAL PRICES. Washington: GPO, 1943. Color. 69 x 53. R.

601. STILL / MORE / PRODUCTION. Washington: War Production Board, 1942. Color. 26 x 18. Bl.

602. STOP 'EM OVER THERE / NOW / —AND / YOU'LL KEEP 'EM AWAY / FROM HERE / JOIN THE FIGHT FOR FREEDOM COMMITTEE NOW. C. C. Beall, artist. Color. 83 x 59. Bl. (Fig. 6.)

WW II: UNITED STATES

603. Same as 602. 36 x 26. Bl.

604. STRONG IN THE STRENGTH OF THE LORD / WE WHO FIGHT IN THE PEOPLE'S CAUSE / WILL NEVER STOP UNTIL THAT CAUSE IS WON. David Stone Martin, artist. Washington: Office of War Information, no. 8, 1942. Color. 71 x 56. Bl.

605. TAKE / CARE! / IDLE HANDS / WORK / FOR HITLER. Washington: War Production Board, 1942. Color. 72 x 51. R.

606. Same as 605. Bl.

607. TEN YEARS AGO: / THE NAZIS BURNED / THESE BOOKS / . . . BUT FREE AMERICANS / CAN STILL READ THEM. Washington: Office of War Information, no. 66, 1943. Color. 71 x 51.

608. THE BATTLE-WISE / INFANTRYMAN . . . / . . . IS CAREFUL / OF WHAT HE SAYS OR WRITES / HOW ABOUT YOU? Jes Wilhelm Schlaikjer, artist. Washington: GPO, 1944. Color. 70 x 50. R.

609. THE / ENEMY / IS LISTENING / HE WANTS TO KNOW / WHAT YOU KNOW / KEEP IT TO YOURSELF. Washington: Office of Facts and Figures. Color. 72 x 51. R.

610. THE FIVE SULLIVAN BROTHERS / "MISSING IN ACTION" OFF THE SOLOMONS / THEY DID THEIR PART. Washington: Office of War Information, no. 42, 1943. Color. 103 x 73. Bl.

611. THE M-1 DOES MY TALKING! / ARE YOU CAREFUL / WHAT YOU SAY OR WRITE? Jes Wilhelm Schlaikjer, artist. Washington: U. S. War Department, 1945. Color. 51 x 37. R.

612. THE MORE WOMEN AT WORK / THE SOONER WE WIN! / WOMEN ARE NEEDED ALSO AS: / . . . SEE YOUR LOCAL U. S. EMPLOYMENT SERVICE. Washington: Office of War Information, no. 52, 1943. Color. 56 x 36. R.

613. THE PRESENT WITH A FUTURE / WAR BONDS. Washington: U. S. Treasury Department, War Savings Staff, 1942. Color. 71 x 56.

614. THE SOUND / THAT KILLS / . . . / DON'T MURDER MEN WITH IDLE WORDS. Ericson, artist. Washington: Office of

War Information, Graphics Division, no. 1, 1942. Color. 51 x 37. R.

615. ... THE STATE OF THIS NATION IS GOOD / THE HEART OF THIS NATION IS SOUND / THE SPIRIT OF THIS NATION IS STRONG / THE FAITH OF THIS NATION IS ETERNAL. / FRANKLIN D. ROOSEVELT / FROM HIS MESSAGE TO CONGRESS, JANUARY 7, 1943. Washington: Office of War Information, no. 40, 1943. Color. 36 x 51. Bl.

616. THE UNITED NATIONS FIGHT FOR FREEDOM / UNITED STATES . . S. Broder, artist. Washington: Office of War Information, no. 19, 1942. Color. 103 x 73. Bl.

617. Same as 616. 71 x 56. Bl.

618. THEY CHEER! / WHEN YOU ARE INATTENTIVE! Directorate of Air Traffic and Safety and Directorate of Safety Education. Color. 43 x 56. Bl.

619. THEY CHEER / WHEN YOU DON'T CHECK YOUR GAS. Directorate of Air Traffic and Safety and Directorate of Safety Education. Color. 43 x 56. Bl.

620. THEY CHEER / WHEN YOU DON'T FASTEN YOUR / SAFETY BELT. Directorate of Air Traffic and Safety and Directorate of Safety Education. Color. 43 x 56. Bl.

621. THEY CHEER / WHEN YOU DON'T MAINTAIN FLYING SPEED! Directorate of Air Traffic and Safety and Directorate of Safety Education. Color. 43 x 56. Bl.

622. THEY CHEER / WHEN YOU FORGET TO LOWER YOUR LANDING GEAR! Directorate of Air Traffic and Safety and Directorate of Safety Education. Color. 43 x 56. Bl.

623. THEY CHEER / WHEN YOU FORGET YOUR MAPS. Directorate of Air Traffic and Safety and Directorate of Safety Education. Color. 43 x 56. Bl.

624. THEY CHEER / WHEN YOU HEDGE-HOP! Directorate of Air Traffic and Safety and Directorate of Safety Education. Color. 43 x 56. Bl.

625. THEY CHEER / WHEN YOU IGNORE / THE RED LINED SPEED! Directorate of Air Traffic and Safety and Directorate of Safety Education. Color. 43 x 56. Bl.

626. THEY CHEER / WHEN YOU JAM ON YOUR BRAKES! Directorate of Air Traffic and Safety and Directorate of Safety Education. Color. 43 x 56. Bl.

627. THEY CHEER / WHEN YOU NEVER USE FLAPS! Directorate of Air Traffic and Safety and Directorate of Safety Education. Color. 43 x 56. Bl.

628. THEY CHEER / WHEN YOU PAY NO ATTENTION TO PATTERN. Directorate of Air Traffic and Safety and Directorate of Safety Education. Color. 43 x 56. Bl.

629. THEY CHEER / WHEN YOU PAY / NO ATTENTION / TO TELEPHONE WIRES. Directorate of Air Traffic and Safety and Directorate of Safety Education. Color. 43 x 56. Bl.

630. THEY CHEER! / WHEN YOU TAKE OFF WITHOUT A WARM-UP!! Directorate of Air Traffic and Safety and Directorate of Safety Education. Color. 43 x 56. Bl.

631. THEY / CHEER / WHEN YOU TAKE OFF WITHOUT LOOKING! Directorate of Air Traffic and Safety and Directorate of Safety Education. Color. 43 x 56. Bl.

632. THEY CHEER! / WHEN YOU TRY FOOLHARDY STUNTS! Directorate of Air Traffic and Safety and Directorate of Safety Education. Color. 43 x 56. Bl.

633. THEY CHEER / WHEN YOU USE NO ALTITUDE! Directorate of Air Traffic and Safety and Directorate of Safety Education. Color. 43 x 56. Bl.

634. THEY'LL LET US KNOW / WHEN TO QUIT! Lyman Anderson, artist. Washington: War Manpower Commission, 1944. Color. 71 x 51. R.

635. THEY'RE CLOSER / THAN YOU THINK! Washington: U. S. Army, Ordnance Department, 1942. Color. 102 x 72. R.

636. THEY'VE GOT MORE IMPORTANT / PLACES TO GO THAN YOU! . . . / SAVE RUBBER / CHECK YOUR TIRES NOW. Walter Richards, artist. Washington: Office of War Information, no. 21, 1942. Color. 103 x 73. Bl.

637. THIS HAPPENS / EVERY 3 MINUTES / STAY ON THE JOB / AND GET IT OVER. Washington: U. S. Army, 1945. Color. 94 x 67. R. (Fig. 58.)

638. THIS IS THE ENEMY. Washington: Office of War Information, no. 76, 1943. Color. 71 x 51.

639. THIS MAN MAY DIE / IF YOU TALK TOO MUCH. Sarra, artist. Washington: Office of War Information, no. 6, 1943. Color. 103 x 73. Bl.

640. Same as 639. 71 x 56. B.

641. TILL WE MEET AGAIN / BUY WAR BONDS. Washington: GPO, 1942. Color. 71 x 56. Bl.

642. TIME IS SHORT. Washington: Office for Emergency Management, Division of Information, 1941. Color. 43 x 290. [Banner].

643. TO HAVE AND TO HOLD / BUY WAR BONDS. Washington: U. S. Treasury Department, War Finance Division, 1944. Color. 102 x 72. Re.

644. TO HAVE / AND TO HOLD! / WAR BONDS. Washington: U. S. Treasury Department, War Finance Division, 1944. Color. 71 x 51. Re.

645. TOOLS ARE WEAPONS / . . . TREAT 'EM RIGHT / . . . Washington: GPO, 1943. Color. 104 x 69. R.

646. TWICE A PATRIOT / EX-PRIVATE OBIE BARTLETT LOST LEFT ARM—PEARL HARBOR— / RELEASED DEC., 1941—NOW AT WORK WELDING / IN A WEST COAST SHIPYARD . . . / "SOMETIMES I FEEL MY JOB HERE IS / AS IMPORTANT AS THE ONE I HAD TO LEAVE." Washington: War Production Board, 1943. Color. 102 x 72. R. (Fig. 49.)

647. UNCLE SAM / SETS THE / BEST / TABLE / CHIP IN FOR THE CHOW / BUY WAR BONDS / NOW. . . . / CONTRIBUTED TO THE QUARTERMASTER CORPS BY THE MAKERS OF ALKA-SELTZER. G. W. French, artist. 1944. Color. 102 x 67. R.

648. U.S.O. CAMP SHOWS / (MOTION PICTURES DIVISION) / PRESENT / THROUGH THE FACILITIES OF /

AMERICAN OVERSEAS ARTISTS / AN ALL STAR SHOW / WITH KAY FRANCIS / MARTHA RAYE / CAROLE LANDIS / MITZI MAYFAIR / AT THIS CAMP. [Great Britain]. Color. 76 x 51. Sm.

649. USO / UNTIL THEY'RE HOME / NATIONAL WAR FUND. Hayden Hayden, artist. Color. 54 x 36. H.

650. UNITED / WE ARE STRONG / UNITED WE WILL WIN. H. Koerner, artist. Washington: Office of War Information, no. 64, 1943. Color. 102 x 72. By.

651. UNITED YUGOSLAV RELIEF FUND / OF AMERICA. New York: United Friends of Yugoslavia, Inc. Color. 56 x 36. H.

652. URGENT / NOTICE / 1. FIGHTING MEN AND MATERIALS ARE BEING SHIFTED / FOR FINAL PHASES OF THE WAR WITH JAPAN / .... Washington: GPO, 1945. Color. 67 x 45. R.

653. USE IT UP—WEAR IT OUT— / MAKE IT DO! / OUR LABOR AND OUR GOODS ARE FIGHTING. Washington: Office of War Information, no. 39, 1943. Color. 71 x 55. R.

654. VETERANS / JOBS IN THE FEDERAL / GOVERNMENT ARE OPEN TO YOU / YOU GET PREFERENCE IN APPOINTMENT / FOR FULL INFORMATION / .... Victor Beals, artist. Washington: U. S. Civil Service Commission, 1944. Color. 51 x 37. R.

655. "VICTORY THROUGH AIRPOWER—PEACE THROUGH AIRPOWER" Lockheed Aircraft Corporation-Vega Aircraft Corporation. Color. 43 x 41. By.

656. WANTED! / FOR MURDER / HER CARELESS TALK COSTS LIVES. Victor Keppler, artist. Washington: Office of War Information, 1944. Color. 72 x 51. R.

657. WAR RELIEF / GIVE! / AMERICAN RED CROSS. F. Brunner, artist. American Red Cross. Color. 51 x 33.

658. WAR TRAFFIC MUST / COME FIRST / DON'T WASTE TRANSPORTATION / ASSOCIATION OF AMERICAN RAILROADS IN COOPERATION WITH THE OFFICE OF DEFENSE TRANSPORTATION. Fred Chance, artist. Color. 46 x 36. R.

659. WARNING! / . . . WHOEVER, IN TIME OF WAR, WITH / INTENT THAT THE SAME SHALL BE COMMUNI- /CATED TO THE ENEMY. . . . Washington: GPO. Color. 51 x 36. R.

660. WE ARE FIGHTING / THE AXIS / NOT EACH OTHER. B & W. 35 x 43. M.

661. WE ARE READY★WHAT ABOUT YOU? / JOIN THE / SCHOOLS AT WAR / PROGRAM / . . . Irving Nurick, artist. Washington: U. S. Treasury Department, 1942. Color. 71 x 56. Bl.

662. WE CAN . . . / WE WILL . . . / WE MUST! / . . . FRANKLIN D. ROOSEVELT / BUY U. S. WAR SAVINGS BONDS & STAMPS NOW. Washington: GPO, 1942. Color. 29 x 53. Bl.

663. WE CLEAR THE WAY / THE CORPS OF / ENGINEERS / UNITED STATES ARMY. Jes Wilhelm Schlaikjer, artist. Washington: U. S. War Department, 1942. Color. 64 x 31. R.

664. "WE CONSIDER PEACE A CATASTROPHE / FOR HUMAN CIVILIZATION." / —MUSSOLINI / WHAT DO YOU SAY: AMERICA? Washington: Office of War Information, Graphics Division, 1942. Color. 51 x 35. R.

665. WE HAVE JUST BEGUN / TO FIGHT! / PEARL HARBOR / BATAAN / CORAL SEA / MIDWAY / GUADACANAL / NEW GUINEA / BISMARCK SEA / CASABLANCA / ALGIERS / TUNISIA. Washington: Office of War Information, no. 62, 1943. Color. 57 x 41. R.

666. WE HAVE NOT A MINUTE TO LOSE / IN ALL OUR OPERATIONS, WHETHER IN AFRICA, / OUT OF ENGLAND, IN ASIA OR THE PACIFIC, THE SUPPLY OF / THE MEN WHO ARE DOING THE FIGHTING IS A VITAL FACTOR. / THIS IS YOUR RESPONSIBILITY— AND WE HAVE NOT A SINGLE / MINUTE TO LOSE. WE MUST NOT FAIL THE MEN WHO / ARE DOING THE FIGHTING. / G. C. MARSHALL, U.S.A., CHIEF OF STAFF. Washington: U. S. Army, Services of Supply Depots, 1943. Color. 68 x 54.

667. ... WE HERE HIGHLY RESOLVE THAT THESE DEAD / SHALL NOT HAVE DIED IN VAIN ... / REMEMBER DEC. 7TH! Washington: Office of War Information, no. 14, 1942. Color. 71 x 56. Bl.

668. "WE SHALL SOON HAVE OUR / STORM TROOPERS IN AMERICA!" / —HITLER / WHAT DO YOU SAY, AMERICA? Washington: Office of War Information, Graphics Division, 1942. Color. 51 x 35. R. (Fig. 51.)

669. "WE'LL HAVE LOTS TO EAT THIS / WINTER, WON'T WE MOTHER? / GROW YOUR OWN / CAN YOUR OWN. A. Parker, artist. Washington: Office of War Information, no. 57, 1943. Color. 58 x 41. R. (Fig. 53.)

670. WE'LL TAKE CARE OF / THE RISING SUN / YOU TAKE CARE OF RISING PRICES / .... Washington: Office of Economic Stabilization. Color. 56 x 42. R.

671. WHEN YOU'RE / A.W.O.L. / YOU'RE WORKING / FOR / THE AXIS. Washington: War Production Board, 1942. Color. 103 x 73. Bl.

672. Same as 671. B.

673. WHERE OUR MEN ARE FIGHTING / OUR FOOD IS FIGHTING / BUY WISELY—COOK CAREFULLY—STORE CAREFULLY—USE LEFTOVERS. Washington: GPO, 1943. Color. 71 x 56. Bl.

674. "WHERE SKILL / AND COURAGE COUNT" / SIGNAL CORPS / UNITED STATES ARMY. Jes Wilhelm Schlaikjer, artist. Washington: U. S. War Department, Bureau of Public Relations, 1942. Color. 64 x 49. R.

675. WHO WANTS TO KNOW? / SILENCE MEANS SECURITY. Washington: U. S. War Department, Adjutant General's Office, 1943. Color. 56 x 36. R.

676. WITHOUT RATIONING / RATIONING MEANS / A FAIR SHARE FOR ALL OF US / WITH RATIONING. Washington: Office of Price Administration, 1943. Color. 71 x 56. Bl.

677. WOMEN / IN THE WAR / WE CAN'T WIN / WITHOUT THEM. Washington: War Manpower Commission, 1942. Color. 102 x 72. R. (Fig. 50.)

678. WOMEN / THERE'S WORK TO BE DONE / AND A WAR TO BE WON . . . / NOW! / SEE YOUR U. S. EMPLOYMENT SERVICE. Vernon Grant, artist. Washington: War Manpower Commission, 1944. Color. 51 x 36. R.

679. "WON'T YOU GIVE MY BOY / A CHANCE TO GET HOME?" / DON'T TRAVEL—UNLESS / YOUR TRIP HELPS WIN THE WAR. Jerome Rozen, artist. Washington: Office of Defense Transportation, 1944. Color. 68 x 51. R.

680. WORK ON A FARM . . . / THIS SUMMER / JOIN THE U. S. CROP CORPS / SEE YOUR U. S. EMPLOYMENT SERVICE OR YOUR LOCAL COUNTY AGENT. Douglas, artist. Washington: Office of War Information, no. 59, 1943. Color. 58 x 41. R.

681. WORLD WAR II IN THE NORTH SEA AREA . . . / NAVY WAR MAP / NO. 3 . . . Washington: U. S. Navy. Color. 103 x 150. Bl.

682. YOU ARE NEEDED NOW / JOIN THE / ARMY NURSE CORPS / APPLY AT YOUR RED CROSS RECRUITING STATION. Ruzzie Green, artist. 1943. Color. 79 x 52. R.

683. "YOU BUY 'EM / WE'LL FLY 'EM!" / DEFENSE / BONDS / STAMPS. Wilkinsons, artist. Color. 36 x 26. Bl.

684. YOU CAN'T AFFORD / TO MISS EITHER! / BUY BONDS EVERY PAYDAY. Martha Sawyers, artist. Washington: U. S. Treasury Department, War Finance Division, 1944. Color. 97 x 76. R.

685. Same as 684. 71 x 57. R.

686. Same as 684. 36 x 28. R.

687. YOU DISH IT UP / WE'LL DISH IT OUT / THE BEST FED SOLDIER / IN THE WORLD / THANKS TO YOU AND THE QUARTERMASTER CORPS / COMPLIMENTS OF ALKA-SELTZER. G. W. French, artist. Color. 102 x 67. R.

688. YOU DON'T HAVE TO / DIG FOR / GOLD / WRITE A / SUGGESTION. Washington: Army Service Forces, suggestion poster no. 6, 1944. Color. 33 x 24. R.

689. YOU KNOCK 'EM OUT— / WE'LL KNOCK 'EM DOWN / MORE PRODUCTION. John Falter, artist. Washington: War Production Board, 1942. Color. 102 x 72. R.

690. YOU, TOO, ARE / NEEDED IN A / WAR JOB / WORK IN A / FOOD PROCESSING PLANT / (FULL OR PART TIME). Frank Bensing, artist. Washington: War Manpower Commission, 1945. Color. 51 x 37. R.

691. YOUR COUNTRY / EXPECTS YOU TO: / 1. TAKE CARE OF EQUIPMENT . . . / . . . / YOUR CARE MAY SAVE THE / LIFE OF A COUNTRYMAN. Washington: War Production Board, 1942. Color. 72 x 52. R.

692. YOUR FLEET / GUARANTEES FREEDOM / NAVY DAY / OCTOBER 27, 1944. Washington: Bureau of Naval Personnel, Navy Recruiting Service, 1944. Color. 103 x 88. R.

693. YOUR GOVERNMENT WARNS / PREPARE FOR / WINTER / NOW! / TAKE DEALER'S ADVICE— / . . . / CHECK YOUR HEATING PLANT— / . . . / "WINTERIZE" YOUR HOME— / . . . FUEL IS SCARCE. CONSERVE IT! Washington: Solid Fuels Administration for War, 1944. Color. 71 x 51. R.

694. YOUR JOB IS TO / KEEP 'EM SHOOTING! H. M. Stoops, artist. Washington: U. S. Army, Ordnance Department, 1942. Color. 102 x 72.

695. YOUR PEN . . . AN ENEMY WEAPON? / NOT IF YOU KEEP WHAT YOU / KNOW TO YOURSELF! / WATCH WHAT YOU WRITE. Washington: U. S. Army, Recruiting Publicity Bureau, 1943. Color. 70 x 47. P.

696. YOUR SCRAP / . . . BROUGHT IT DOWN / KEEP SCRAPING / IRON AND STEEL-RUBBER / ALL OTHER METALS-RAGS / MOVE ALL SCRAP NOW! S. Broder, artist. Washington: GPO, 1942. Color. 71 x 51. Bl.

697. YOUR SUGGESTIONS / HELP HIM . . . / AND YOU / WIN $5 TO $250.00 / HAND IN YOUR SUGGESTIONS / EVEN SMALL / SUGGESTIONS / SPEED PLANS / AND SUPPLIES / THAT TURN THE / TIDE OF VICTORY. Washington: U. S. Army, 1944. Color. 51 x 36. R.

INDEX OF ARTISTS

[Numbers refer to posters in the INVENTORY.]

WORLD WAR I

CANADA

    Sampson: 5

FRANCE

    Adler, Jules: 19
    Boursset, Firmen: 17
    Capon, Georges: 14
    Chavannaz, B.: 8, 20, 48
    Courboin: 45
    Delaspre, H.: 29
    Dorival, Georges: 14
    Faivre, Jules Abel: 13, 28, 33, 35, 43
    Falter, M.: 36
    Flot, Louis: 21
    Hansi [Jean Jacques Waltz] :18
    Jonas, Lucien-Hector: 9, 12, 22, 30
    Lavaire, Germaine: 46
    LeLong, A.: 39
    Leroux, Auguste: 11, 44
    Mourgue: 27
    Naudin, Bernard: 26
    Neumont, Maurice: 15, 25, 34
    Outz, M. Richard: 42
    Picard, G.: 23
    Pichon, Atetien: 36
    Poulbot, Francisque: 16, 24, 38
    Reson, Georges: 37
    Steinlen, Theophile-Alexandre: 32, 41
    Waltz, Jean Jacques [Hansi] : 18
    Willette, Adolphe Leon: 10, 47

GREAT BRITAIN

    Bassano: 73, 74
    Foy, D. D.: 72
    Fry, W. A.: 96
    Good, Gerald: 70
    Kealey, E. V.: 51, 61, 62
    Kemp-Welsh, Lucy Elizabeth: 63
    Lipscombe, Guy: 53, 69
    Low, Baron: 59
    Meyers, Lloyd: 54
    Parkridge, Bernard: 83
    Paxter: 99
    Powell, Sir R. S. S. Baden: 50
    Soutary, V.: 52
    Wood, Charles: 91
    Wood, Lawson: 113

UNITED STATES

    A. R. B.: 160
    Baldridge, C. LeRoy: 193, 206
    Bancroft, Milton: 136
    Benda, W. T.: 232
    Beneker, Gerrit A.: 207
    Blashfield, E. H.: 133
    Bracker, M. Leone: 173
    Britton, L. N.: 212
    Bull, Charles Livingston: 174

INDEX OF ARTISTS

Christy, Howard Chandler: 128, 137, 214
Coffin, Haskell: 169, 217
Cozz: 215
Craig, Wilson: 186
Dewey: 189
Emerson, Caspar, Jr.: 158
Everett, Walter H.: 180
Fisher, Harrison C.: 150, 166
Flagg, James Montgomery: 165, 213, 220
Foringer, Alonzo Earl: 195
Grant, Gordon: 228
Green, H. R.: 183
Grosse, J. L.: 154
J. M. H.: 197
Harris, Laurence S.: 146
Illian, George: 175
Ingres, Maurice: 178
Kidder: 152
King, W. B.: 161
Krieghoft, C.: 221
Leyendecker, Joseph Christian: 222
Liello, J.: 121
Lynch, V.: 114
Orr, Alfred Everitt: 144
Paus, Herbert: 155, 205, 218
Pennell, Joseph: 194, 209
Porteous, R. H.: 231
Raemaekers, Louis: 135
Raleigh, Henry Patrick: 147, 164
Richards, G. M.: 187
Riesenberg, Sidney H.: 190
Rogers, W. A.: 188
St. John, J. Allen: 210
Sheridan, J. F.: 143
Smith, Dan: 127, 153, 176
Smith, Jessie Willcox: 148
Stahr, Paul: 118
Stern: 115, 116

Sterner, Albert: 224
Still, Roy Hull: 208
Strothmann, F.: 119
Tyng, Griswold: 200
Verrees, J. Paul: 126, 172
Whitehead, Walter: 131
Williams, J. Scott: 145
Wright, George: 141
Young, Ellsworth: 198

WORLD WAR II

CANADA

Arbuckle, Franklin: 239
Casson, A. J.: 246
Jameson, L. B.: 258
Leonard, Jac: 238
McLarell, Al: 242
Morris, G. R.: 255
Nichol: 245
Rae, G. M.: 243
Rogers, Hubert: 253
Sampson: 257
Trevor, L.: 250

FRANCE

Carlu, Jean: 263

GERMANY

Ahrens: 413
Blossfield, Karl: 280
Dill, S. Siehard: 266
Freres, W.: 268
Friedrich, E. W.: 278
Fuchs: 345
Gotz, E.: 277, 281
Henzler: 269

INDEX OF ARTISTS

Hoyer: 382, 388, 389, 391
Jager, P. K.: 282
Kleine, Willi: 291, 293, 305, 310, 314, 325, 326
Knabe: 404, 405, 406, 410, 412
Mann, Land Wehr: 287
Rusch, Ernst: 288
Wittig-Friesen: 372, 373, 376, 381, 383, 387, 393, 394, 411

GREAT BRITAIN

Gardner, James: 417
Stone, Marc: 420
Wooton: 421

UNITED STATES

Anderson, Harry: 434
Anderson, Lyman: 634
Arens: 479
Atherton, John: 430
Barclay, McClelland: 585
Beall, C. C.: 589, 602
Beals, Victor: 654
Bendix, W. T.: 572
Bensing, Frank: 690
Bingham: 558
Broder, S.: 447, 616, 696
Brunner, F.: 657
Carlson, C. X.: 555
Carlu, Jean: 435
Chaliapin, Boris: 442
Chance, Fred: 658
Crockwell, Douglass: 438
Daugherty, J.: 544
Dohanos, Stevan: 441, 487, 504
Dorne, Albert: 433, 535, 547, 596
Douglas: 680
Eah-Ha-Wa: 454

Edmundson: 481
Ericson: 614
Falter, John: 500, 517, 689
Fischer, Anton Otto: 426, 428
Fitzpatrick: 478
Flagg, James Montgomery: 515, 516
French, G. W.: 647, 687
Gaydos: 459
Grant, Vernon: 678
Graves, Stu: 579
Green, Ruzzie: 682
Guignon, Henri: 511
Ha a tee Ben: 454
Hayden, Hayden: 649
Helguera, Leon: 463
Keppler, Victor: 656
Koerner, H.: 584, 650
Martin, David Stone: 604
Meyers, Nancy Morse: 514
Munsett: 493
Nichols, Ruth: 575
Noxon: 509
Nurick, Irving: 661
Parker, A.: 483, 669
Perlin, Bernard: 440, 536, 587
Prohaska, Ray: 457
Richards, Walter: 636
Riggs: 593
Rockwell, Norman: 542, 550, 565, 566, 568, 581, 582
Rolse: 534
Ross, Alex: 432
Rozen, Jerome: 486, 679
Sarra: 499, 519, 639
Sawyers, Martha: 460, 461, 541, 684
Schlaikjer, Jes Wilhelm: 465, 512, 524, 546, 551, 560, 562, 578, 586, 594, 608, 611, 663, 674
Schreiber, Georges: 522, 530

INDEX OF ARTISTS

Siebel: 597
Sloan, Robert: 473
Smith, Lawrence: 476
Stoops, H. M.: 694
Strong, Grover: 505
von Schmidt, Harold: 506, 527
Warren, Ferdinand: 439
White, Elmo: 525
Wiley, Dick: 489
Wilkinsons: 683
Williams, Dick: 561
Williams, F.: 475
Woodburn, Tom B.: 595